How Federal Is the Constitution?

American Enterprise Institute
for Public Policy Research

A DECADE OF STUDY OF THE CONSTITUTION

HOW DEMOCRATIC IS THE CONSTITUTION?
Robert A. Goldwin and William A. Schambra, editors

HOW CAPITALISTIC IS THE CONSTITUTION?
Robert A. Goldwin and William A. Schambra, editors

HOW DOES THE CONSTITUTION SECURE RIGHTS?
Robert A. Goldwin and William A. Schambra, editors

SEPARATION OF POWERS: DOES IT STILL WORK?
Robert A. Goldwin and Art Kaufman, editors

HOW FEDERAL IS THE CONSTITUTION?
Robert A. Goldwin and William A. Schambra, editors

How Federal Is the Constitution?

*Robert A. Goldwin
and William A. Schambra
editors*

American Enterprise Institute for Public Policy Research
Washington D.C.

This book is the fifth in a series in AEI's project "A Decade of Study of the Constitution," funded in part by grants from the National Endowment for the Humanities. A full list of the titles appears on the series page.

"The Idea of the Nation," by Samuel Beer, is reprinted by permission of *The New Republic*, © 1982, The New Republic, Inc.

Distributed by arrangement with

UPA, Inc.
4720 Boston Way   3 Henrietta Street
Lanham, MD 20706   London WC2E 8LU England

Library of Congress Cataloging-in-Publication Data

How federal is the constitution?

(Constitutional studies / American Enterprise
Institute) (AEI studies ; 454)
"This book is the fifth in a series in AEI's project "A decade of study of the constitution"—T.p. verso.
Contents: Federalism and the dilemma of popular government / Edward C. Banfield—The Constitution/
William Jeffrey, Jr.—Our thoroughly federal Constitution / Daniel J. Elazar—[etc.]
1. Federal government—United States. 2. United States—Constitutional history. I. Goldwin, Robert A., 1922– . II. Schambra, William A. III. Series: Constitutional studies. IV. Series: AEI studies ; 454.
JK325.H67 1986   321.02'0973   86-32221

ISBN 0-8447-3619-8
ISBN 0-8447-3618-x (pbk.)

AEI Studies 454   *Printed in the United States of America*

88 - 2337

Contents

The Editors and the Authors

ROBERT A. GOLDWIN is resident scholar and codirector of constitutional studies at the American Enterprise Institute. He has served in the White House as special consultant to the president and, concurrently, as adviser to the secretary of defense. He has taught at the University of Chicago and at Kenyon College and was dean of St. John's College in Annapolis. He is the editor of a score of books on American politics, coeditor of the AEI series of volumes on the Constitution, and author of numerous articles, including "Of Men and Angels: A Search for Morality in the Constitution" and "How to Read the Original Constitution on Subjects It Doesn't Mention."

WILLIAM A. SCHAMBRA is resident fellow at the American Enterprise Institute and codirector of constitutional studies at AEI. He is coeditor, with Robert A. Goldwin, of *How Democratic Is the Constitution?*, *How Capitalistic Is the Constitution?*, and *How Does the Constitution Secure Rights?* and author of "The Roots of the American Public Philosophy" and "Progressive Liberalism and American Community."

EDWARD C. BANFIELD, George D. Markham Professor of Government emeritus at Harvard University, has written extensively on American politics, especially the problems of American cities and political party reform. His books include *City Politics* (with James Q. Wilson), *The Moral Basis of a Backward Society* (with Laura Banfield), and *The Unheavenly City*.

SAMUEL H. BEER is Eaton Professor of the Science of Government, emeritus at Harvard University. A former president of the American Political Science Association, he has written about British government and politics, American federalism, and political philosophy. He has taken an active part in state and national politics, serving as national chairman of Americans for Democratic Action from 1959 to 1962.

DANIEL J. ELAZAR is professor of political science and director of the Center for the Study of Federalism at Temple University, Senator

N. M. Paterson Professor of Political Studies and head of the Institute of Local Government at Bar-Ilan University in Israel, and president of the Jerusalem Institute for Federal Studies. He has written and edited numerous books on American federalism, including *The American Partnership: Federal-State Relations in the Nineteenth Century*, *American Federalism: A View from the States*, and *Cities of the Prairie*; he is also editor of *Publius: The Journal of Federalism*.

WILLIAM JEFFREY, JR., was, at the time of his death, professor of law at the University of Cincinnati Law School. He was co-author, with William Winslow Crosskey, of volume III of *Politics and the Constitution in the History of the United States*. A number of his articles have appeared in law journals, including "Letters of 'Brutus': A Neglected Element in the Ratification Campaign of 1787–88," and "Early American Court Records: A Bibliography of Printed Materials."

DAVID M. KENNEDY is professor of American history at Stanford University. He is the author of *Birth Control in America: The Career of Margaret Sanger*, which was awarded the Bancroft Prize, and *Over Here: The First World War and American Society*. His most recent books are *Power and Responsibility: Case Studies in American Leadership* and *The American Pageant: A History of the Republic*.

GARY L. MCDOWELL is associate director of the Office of Public Affairs at the U.S. Department of Justice. He is the author of *Equity and the Constitution* and *Curbing the Courts: The Constitution and the Limits of Judicial Power*; he has also edited several volumes including *The American Founding: Politics, Statesmanship and the Constitution*.

JEAN YARBROUGH is professor of political science and director of the Institute for Political Philosophy and Policy Analysis at Loyola University of Chicago. Her articles on republicanism, federalism, and decentralization in scholarly journals include "Republicanism Reconsidered: Some Thoughts on *The Federalist*'s View of Representation" and "Federalism in the Foundation and Preservation of the American Republic."

Foreword

When President Reagan spoke of the need for a "new federalism" in his first State of the Union address, his proposal was greeted with profound skepticism. There had been, after all, many similar presidential efforts in preceding decades, none of which had had much effect. By 1982, it seemed, the question of the proper balance between national and state governments had long since been settled, and decisively so, in favor of a powerful national government.

It soon became apparent, however, that the federal government faced a number of daunting problems—foremost among them the national deficit—arising in large part precisely from its near monopoly of governing functions and the enormous, unbalanced budgets that it tended to generate. Nonetheless, an array of domestic social problems continued to demand our attention—and the states, to the astonishment of many, rose to the occasion. In education, welfare, job training, industrial revitalization, and trade expansion, the states launched countless new and often innovative programs, while the national government struggled to set its budgetary house in order. Once again, the value of a well-balanced, federal system within our political structure had been demonstrated.

How Federal Is the Constitution? traces the origin of that system back to the founding of the republic and to the debates of that period over the proper balance between the state and national governments. Those debates generated some of the most profound thought available on the federal balance, as on so many other issues. Those original exchanges have echoed through most of the major events of our national history and lie beneath the surface of today's controversy over federalism, as the essays in this volume, representing the major points of view in that controversy, make clear.

AEI is pleased to add this book, during the bicentennial year of our Constitution, to its series of essay volumes illuminating controversies that arose at the time of the founding and that continue to agitate American politics to this day.

CHRISTOPHER C. DEMUTH
President
American Enterprise Institute

Preface

"The question of the relation of the States to the Federal Government is the cardinal question of our constitutional system," Woodrow Wilson wrote in 1908. "At every turn of our national development, we have been brought face to face with it, and no definition either of statesmen or of judges has ever quieted or decided it." Wilson's observation is as valid today as when he made it almost three quarters of a century ago, and it is easy to see why. In most free nations around the world, debates over public policy turn on the question, What is to be done? In the United States, we must ask not only, What is to be done? but additionally and importantly, Who is to do it—local, state, or national government?

The question posed by this volume, How federal is our constitutional system? must be addressed, then, by presidents, legislators, judges, and citizens, before undertaking projects as broad as civil rights legislation, revenue sharing, or welfare reform, or as narrow as the disposal of wastewater. The priority of the federalism question is demonstrated by the prominent role it has played in most of the important political debates throughout our history. The effort to define and preserve the powers of national and state governments respectively was a central issue at the Constitutional Convention in 1787. Federalism clearly was a critical issue in the secession controversy and on both sides in our Civil War. A redefinition of federal and state responsibilities was a central part of Theodore Roosevelt's Square Deal, Franklin Roosevelt's New Deal, and Lyndon Johnson's Great Society. Finally and most recently, President Reagan's New Federalism was an explicit effort to restore an earlier version of federal-state relations.

Why has federalism figured so prominently in our political controversies? To answer that, it is necessary to understand the federalism issue as something considerably more profound than a debate over which level of government can perform which administrative tasks most efficiently. The issue is, in fact, an integral part of some of the most important questions we face as a people, as the essays in this volume should make clear. Is the cause of political liberty served by limiting the authority of the national government? Or do we thereby empower possibly oppressive local majorities, as occurred in the South and elsewhere before and after the Civil War? Does our national commitment to equality demand uniformity in the treatment of all citizens in all respects, regardless of state of residence? Or would we thereby sacrifice the diversity and pluralism that strong states and localities make possible? Is democratic citizenship the product of membership in a national community and service to the "national idea"? Or is citizenship developed by participation in governing at the state and local levels, where public issues are simpler, more easily understood, and thus have a clearer, more immediate bearing on the private interests of individuals?

As we try to answer these questions relating to federalism, we should turn first as Americans to the U.S. Constitution and to the writings of those who drafted and supported it, and of those who opposed it. We do so not out of blind reverence for the Constitution or for the intentions of those who framed it. Indeed, as will become clear in this volume, just what the Constitution and its framers intended with regard to federalism is a source of considerable controversy, open to different—in fact, diametrically opposed—interpretations. Moreover, as the reader will also discover, it is by no means clear how much weight should be placed on the original constitutional design for federalism, after two hundred years of dramatic changes in our economic, political, and social arrangements and in our international situation.

We turn nonetheless to the Constitution and the debates over its ratification because we find there some of the most profound and enduring insights into the issues raised by federalism and the ends it was intended to serve, such as liberty, equality, and the development of democratic citizenship. As long as these principles remain important to Americans, the controversy over federalism and its purposes, as illuminated by the Founding debates, will also be important, and considerably more than a squabble over division of administrative responsibilities. This volume is intended to introduce the reader to that controversy, through essays prepared by leading spokesmen for different viewpoints on such issues as the framers' intentions for federalism, the effects of two hundred years of domestic and international developments on national-state relations, and the ways nation and state may or may not serve ends we consider valuable.

As with all volumes in this series, we hope to place the reader in the middle of a debate that is as lively and important today as it was in 1787, with enough information, persuasively and interestingly presented, to permit the reader to form his or her own judgment on the question. By so aiding citizens to understand better an issue that, as Woodrow Wilson suggested, is unlikely ever to be "quieted or decided," we hope to contribute to the thoughtful observance of the bicentennial of the Constitution of the United States.

ROBERT A. GOLDWIN
WILLIAM A. SCHAMBRA

1

Federalism and the Dilemma of Popular Government

Edward C. Banfield

Beginning with the Truman administration, there have been persistent and sometimes strenuous efforts to devolve many federal activities to state and local governments.[1] These efforts have almost entirely failed. Meanwhile, the number and variety of federal interventions in what until recently were generally considered local matters has increased at an accelerating rate. Federal domestic spending more than doubled as a percentage of gross national product in the twenty-five years before 1980.

The endeavor to reduce the federal government's domestic role moves along three lines: transfer of programs to the states, relaxation of conditions attached to grants, and imposition of a fixed limit on federal spending. Curiously there has been almost no effort to find and set forth some general principles that will define and limit the legitimate sphere of government, especially of the federal government. (The Advisory Commission for Intergovernmental Relations proposed in 1980 that the president convene key federal, state, and local officials to discuss—among other things—"what the term 'national purpose' now means in a regulatory and programmatic sense," but nothing came of this.)[2]

The reason for this inattention to principles may be that practical people sense that an effort to agree on principles sufficiently definite to serve as criteria, or to implement them if they are agreed on, would be both futile and divisive. Americans are accustomed to thinking of their government as a limited one; the doctrine of limited government was, as Herbert J. Storing wrote, "the great principle of the revolution."[3] But they are also accustomed to thinking that government ought to serve the people in whatever ways they want, and—as the vastness of the federal establishment testifies—they approve, tacitly

1

at least, of political arrangements that bring government into almost every aspect of life.

The import of this thinking is that it is futile to try to limit government to some defined sphere. Nothing of importance can be done to stop the spread of federal power, let alone to restore something like the division of powers agreed upon by the Framers of the Constitution. The reason lies in human nature: men cannot be relied upon voluntarily to abide by their agreements, including those upon which their political order depends. There is an antagonism, amounting to an incompatibility, between popular government—meaning government in accordance with the will of the people—and the maintenance of limits on the sphere of government. This fact, clearly recognized by Thomas Hobbes, John Locke, and many later writers, constitutes "the dilemma of popular government."[4]

In brief, the argument is that leading figures at the Convention of 1787 saw the failure of state governments and of the government (if it can be called that) existing under the Articles of Confederation as resulting from the unwillingness of individuals and of state governments to subordinate their special interests to the general interest; that—judged by the intentions of these leading figures—the Convention itself failed from this same cause; that Madison thought (or affected to think) that the structure of the new government might enable it to escape the dilemma; that the agreement the framers reached on the division of powers was immediately breached by the leaders among them; that during fifty years of "elite democracy" the powers of the federal government were much enlarged; and, finally, that the pressures of pluralistic democracy subsequently eroded most of the remaining limits on federal power.

Government by the People

The dilemma of popular government brought the framers together in Philadelphia on May 18, 1787. The great principle proclaimed in the Declaration of Independence—that governments derive their just powers from the consent of the governed—had been made the basis of state constitutions during the Revolution. In the 1780s, it appeared that the revolutionary principle had not worked and perhaps could not be made to work. The federation of states organized under the Articles of Confederation had driven George Washington almost to distraction during the war; it was manifestly incapable of coping with the great problems of the new nation—stabilization of money and credit, foreign affairs, the disposal of public lands, and the rest. Washington, Alexander Hamilton, James Madison, Benjamin Franklin, James

Wilson, Gouverneur Morris, and others thought it obvious that a national government exercising its power upon people, rather than upon states, was urgently and indispensably needed. "The primary source of all our disorders," Washington wrote, "lies in the different State Governments, and in the tenacity of that power which pervades the whole of their systems."[5]

The power to which he referred was popular government or, as some saw it, democracy run riot. To Madison and some others the need to protect people from capricious and unjust state governments was as compelling as that to create a power capable of dealing with national interests. The failures and the injustices of state governments, Madison said, were "so frequent and so flagrant as to alarm the most steadfast friends of Republicanism." These evils, more than anything else, had produced the uneasiness that led to the Convention and prepared the public mind for a general reform.[6] Under the sway of popular leaders ("local demagogues," the nationalists called them), the state legislatures passed paper money, legal tender, debt installment, and other laws serving dominant interests—debtors or creditors, merchants, or members of a religious sect—without regard to people's rights or to the general interest of the society.[7] The powers of government exercised by the people "swallowed up the other branches," Edmund Randolph told the Convention; none of the state constitutions had provided sufficient checks against democracy. In tracing to their origins the evils under which the United States labored, he said, every man had found there "the turbulence and follies of democracy."[8]

Some of the nationalists wanted to abolish the states entirely. That, however, was politically impossible. In presenting to the Convention the Virginia Plan (in which, incidentally, the word "national" appeared no fewer than nineteen times), Randolph proposed that the idea of states be "nearly annihilated."[9] Madison, the principal drafter of the plan that Randolph presented, had in mind a way to end state influence. It was to give the national government a veto over state laws. The necessity of a general government, he said, arose from the propensity of the states to pursue their particular interests in opposition to the general interest. Nothing short of a veto on their laws could stop this.[10]

Citizens and governments, it appeared, each presented the dilemma of popular government. Citizens used their freedom in ways that infringed upon the rights of fellow citizens: debtors, for example, used government to cheat their creditors. States used their freedom to serve local interests at the expense of national ones; as Wilson put it, "Each endeavored to cut a slice from the common loaf, to add to his own morsel, till at length the confederation became frittered down . . . ."[11]

In July, the small states asserted their special interest over the national one by demanding equal weight with the large states in the general government. The result was the Great Compromise. Each state legislature would send two representatives to the Senate; in the House representation would be determined by popular vote. The new government would thus be "partly federal, and partly national"—"a composition of both."[12]

To the nationalists, this compromise was a failure. After the compromise committee had made its report, Washington wrote Hamilton: "I *almost* despair of seeing a favorable issue . . . and do therefore repent having had any agency in the business."[13] Madison thought that the union was now "a feudal system of republics," which was hardly better than a "Confederation of independent States." The Constitution, he wrote Jefferson shortly before the Convention adjourned, would "neither effectually *answer* its *national object* nor prevent the local *mischiefs* which everywhere *excites disgusts* ag [ain]st the state governments."[14] Wilson was sensible that perfection was unattainable in any plan; this (an equal voice for the states in the second branch), however, was "a fundamental and a perpetual error."[15]

Popular government in the states had prevented the making of a popular government in the nation. So at least it seemed to Washington. "The men who oppose a strong & energetic government," he wrote Hamilton, "are, in my opinion, narrow minded politicians, or are under the influence of local views."[16]

Madison saw clearly the dilemma of popular government (which, of course, would have existed even if the states had been annihilated). In the Convention debates and later in the first paper that he wrote for *The Federalist*, he grappled with it. The problem for a friend of popular governments, he wrote in *Federalist* 10, is to find a proper cure for the violence of faction "without violating the principle to which he is attached." In other words, it is "to secure both the public good and the rights of other citizens" while preserving "the spirit and the form of popular government."

Faction, which he defined as any combination of citizens acting contrary to the rights of others "or to the permanent and aggregate interests of the community," arose from the natural diversity in the faculties of man, the protection of which (the dilemma again) "is the first object of government."

The problem was not that men were radically selfish (if that were the case, Madison wrote in *Federalist* 55, "nothing less than the chains of despotism can restrain them from destroying and devouring one

4

another"); rather it arose from the diversity of faculties, which produced motives by no means all of which were blameworthy—zeal for opinions and attachments to leaders, for example—but which led to differences and animosities and to the formation of factions. The principal task of legislation was to regulate faction. "But [the dilemma again] what are the different classes of legislators themselves but advocates and parties to the causes which they determine?"

The danger of *majority* faction troubled Madison most. In *Federalist* 10 he acknowledged in two sentences that minority faction might clog administration or even convulse society; it could be defeated, however, by regular vote of the majority. Majority faction, however, was capable of destroying popular government. Here he saw, but did not fully integrate into his argument, a phenomenon that has only recently been rationalized by decision theorists—namely, that men are motivated differently in large groups than in small.[17] Religious and moral motives, which are not adequate to control injustice and violence on the part of individuals, he wrote in *Federalist* 10, "lose their efficacy in proportion to the number combined together, that is [another dilemma] in proportion as their efficacy becomes needful." The point was one that he had elaborated in the Convention:

> In all cases where a majority are united by a common interest or passion, the rights of the minority are in danger. What motives are to restrain them? A prudent regard to the maxim that honesty is the best policy is found by experience to be as little regarded by bodies of men as by individuals. Respect for character is always diminished in proportion to the number among whom the blame or praise is to be divided. Conscience, the only remaining tie is known to be inadequate in individuals; in large numbers, little is to be expected from it.[18]

If moral motives have less effect on men in large bodies than in small ones, one might infer that governments should be small. (Madison acknowledged the logic of this in a later writing; the "more extensive a country, the more insignificant is each individual in his own eyes," a condition that "may be unfavorable to liberty.")[19] Other considerations, however, were of more importance. There being no motives that could be relied upon to restrain a majority, the need was to prevent a majority from having the same passion or interest at the same time or, failing that, to prevent it from uniting to carry out its schemes. This would be impossible in a "pure democracy" (a society consisting of a small number of citizens who assemble and administer the government in person); in such a society there could be no cure for the mischiefs of faction. By contrast, where the sphere of government was extensive, the community would be divided into so great a number of interests and parties that they might be prevented from cohering and acting as a majority.

In the Convention, where he had supported his argument for an extensive government with the claim that there was less faction and oppression in the large states than in the small (delegates from Connecticut and Maryland asserted the opposite),[20] Madison said that an extensive government "was the only defense agst. the inconveniences of democracy consistent with the democratic form of Govt."[21]

In *Federalist* 10 he did not repeat this claim. Here he proposed (as he had in the Convention) an additional device that did not altogether escape the dilemma. This was the creation of a power capable of coercing a faction, including, of course, a majority one. This was the way he had hoped to end faction in the state governments: by virtue of its veto power, the central government would act as a "disinterested and dispassionate umpire" without becoming a tyrant.[22] This, he had told the Convention, "is at once the most mild & certain means of preserving the harmony of the system." Its usefulness could be seen in the example of the British system where the prerogative of the Crown "stifles in the birth every Act of every part tending to discord or encroachment." The prerogative had sometimes been misapplied, to be sure, but Americans did not have the same reason to fear misapplications in their own system.[23]

In *Federalist* 10, the function of the disinterested and dispassionate umpire was to be performed by representatives "whose enlightened and virtuous sentiments render them superior to local prejudices and to schemes of injustice." The public views would be refined and enlarged

> by passing them through the medium of a chosen body of citizens, whose wisdom may best discern the true interest of their country, and whose patriotism and love of justice will be least likely to sacrifice it to temporary or partial considerations.

The public voice, pronounced by such representatives, might be more consonant with the public good than if pronounced by the people themselves. But there was a danger that the wrong sort of people might be elected.

> Men of factious tempers, of local prejudices, or of sinister designs, may, by intrigue, by corruption, or by other means, first obtain the suffrages, and then betray the interests, of the people.

The more extensive the government, Madison went on to argue, the greater the probability that "proper guardians of the public weal" would be elected. Obviously his second device—the exercise of a prerogative by enlightened and virtuous representatives—was not completely reliable.

Madison, like most of the other nationalists, devoted himself to devising institutional arrangements. He was well aware that republican government presupposed a certain degree of public-spiritedness and reverence for authority:[24] "I go," he said, "on this great republican principle, that the people will have virtue and intelligence to select men of virtue and wisdom."[25] For purposes of constitution-making, men had to be taken as they were or, rather, as they would have to be if popular government was to have a chance of succeeding.

In the discussions preceding and during the Convention there was general agreement that the government should have limited powers. The only question was where and how the limits were to be drawn. At the start of the Convention, leading nationalists, among them Randolph and Wilson, thought an enumeration of powers impossible. Madison came to Philadelphia with a "strong prepossession" in favor of defining the limits and powers of the legislature but he soon became convinced that this could not be done.[26] Since it had been agreed that the national government would be sovereign in some matters and the states in others, the national government's powers would have to be specified.

This was done in Article One, Section 8. The powers of the national government, Madison said in *Federalist* 45, were "few and defined." In fact there were eighteen powers, very few of which could properly be called "defined." Some terms, like "necessary and proper" ("to make all Laws which shall be necessary and proper for carrying into Execution the foregoing Powers . . .") could hardly have been more ambiguous. It is impossible to believe that the delegates were not well aware that such language would bear differing constructions. But it is also impossible to believe that they did not expect it to limit the powers of the central government.

Certainly the voters in the ratifying conventions were told that it would do so. Publius gave the voters of New York very positive assurances. "The powers of the government," said *Federalist* 39, "extend to certain enumerated objects only, and leave to the several states a residuary and inviolable sovereignty over all other objects." *Federalist* 41 considered the charge of some opponents of the Constitution that

> the power to lay and collect taxes, duties, imposts and excises, to pay the debts, and provide for the common defense

and general welfare of the United States amounts to an unlimited commission to exercise every power which may be
alleged to be necessary for the common defense or general
welfare.

This interpretation, Publius said, was absurd. "For what purpose
would the enumeration of particular powers be inserted, if these and
all others were meant to be included in the preceding general power?"
In *Federalist* 17 Publius confessed that, allowing for the utmost latitude
to the lover of power which any reasonable man can require, he could
not see how an administrator of the general government could be
tempted to usurp authorities belonging to the states. It would, he
said, always be far easier for state governments to encroach upon the
national one.

Charles Cotesworth Pinckney, addressing the legislature of South
Carolina, gave slave owners assurances as solid as those that Publius
gave the voters of New York. By this settlement, he said, ". . . we
have a security that the general government can never emancipate
them [the slaves], for no such authority is granted; and it is admitted,
on all hands, that the general government has no powers but what
are expressly granted by the Constitution, and all rights not expressed
were reserved by the several states."[27]

That the ratifying conventions might have still further assurance,
the delegates let it be known that they would support amendments
to the Constitution, one of which (it turned out to be the Tenth) would
state explicitly that powers not delegated to the United States were
reserved to the states.

Expanding Federal Power to Promote General Welfare

The ink was not yet dry on the Constitution when its revision began.
Ironically, it was not men of factious temper, local prejudice, or sin-
ister design who did the revising. Rather it was done by men of
"enlightened views and virtuous sentiments"—those who had, albeit
reluctantly, committed themselves to the Great Compromise and urged
it upon the voters.

In his first message to Congress, President Washington proposed
giving assistance to agriculture, commerce, and manufacturing. The
First Congress, sixteen of whose thirty-nine members had been delegates to the Convention, made tariff legislation its first order of
business. The declared purpose of the Tariff Act was certainly constitutional—Congress had power to lay duties and collect revenues—
but this purpose concealed another, the subsidization of particular
occupations and interests, which the Constitution did not authorize.

"Legislative procedure, as contrasted with economic or political theory," the historian of that Congress, E. A. J. Johnson, has written, "simply assumed that the machinery of government ought to be employed to aid importuning interests . . . ."[28]

In 1791, Hamilton, as secretary of the Treasury, proposed that Congress charter a national bank. Thomas Jefferson, asked by Washington for his opinion on the constitutionality of the bill, said that the Convention had voted against giving Congress the very power now claimed, that the word "necessary" (in the "necessary and proper" clause) did not mean "convenient," and that to give it that meaning "would swallow up all the delegated powers, and reduce the whole to one power."[29] Hamilton, in his opinion, said that the Convention had probably not meant to deny Congress the power of incorporation (the records of the Convention, made public many years later, proved Hamilton wrong and Jefferson right),[30] that "necessary" often means "no more than needful, requisite, incidental, useful, or conducive to," and—most important—that the general legislative authority of Congress *implied* the power to create corporations.[31]

Washington accepted Hamilton's opinion, and the federal sphere was thereby enlarged. It was further enlarged by Hamilton's interpretation of the "general welfare" clause. There was no doubt, he wrote in his *Report on Manufactures*, that the clause necessarily embraced "a vast variety of particulars, which are susceptible neither of specification or of definition." Whatever concerns these matters, he said—he mentioned learning, agriculture, manufactures, and commerce—is within the power of Congress to legislate *as far as regards an application of money* and so long as the appropriation be general rather than local in application.[32]

This interpretation prevailed, despite the strenuous objections of Madison, who had become both anti-Hamilton and anti-nationalist. (In *Federalist* 41, it will be recalled, Madison had called such an interpretation absurd). In his *Report on the Virginia Resolutions*, written ten years later, he warned that it would enlarge the powers of the presidency, thus increasing the amount of presidential patronage, which in turn would render elections more important, making them so violent and corrupt that the public might call for a hereditary succession.[33] Much later (1830), he wrote that the general welfare clause had got into the Constitution more or less by accident, or, as he put it, "inattention to the phraseology occasioned doubtless by its identity with the harmless character attached to it in the Instrument [the Articles of Confederation] from which it was borrowed."[34] ("Inattention" seems unlikely in light of the fact that when Morris, a member of the drafting committee, slyly inserted a semi-colon after the words

9

"to lay and collect taxes, duties, imposts and excises"—thus transforming the words that followed, "to pay the debts and provide for the common defence and general welfare of the United States," into a broad grant of power—the semi-colon was replaced with a comma after the trick was discovered.)[35]

The revisers of the Great Compromise were not all nationalists. Jefferson, as Washington's secretary of state, wrote a *Report on the Fisheries*, which suggested that Congress do something, perhaps remit taxes, to aid the fishing industry.[36] As president, he acknowledged making "a blank paper" of the Constitution by purchasing Louisiana, and his secretary of the treasury, Gallatin, originated vast plans for internal improvements. When Gallatin sought to establish a branch bank of the United States, Jefferson, after protesting that the bank is "of the most deadly hostility existing against the principles and form of our Constitution," gave his approval.[37]

When the election of Andrew Jackson ended the line of presidents "of enlightened views and virtuous sentiments," the powers of the United States had been very substantially enlarged without recourse to the amending process that the Constitution provided. (The Eleventh and Twelfth Amendments were not for the purpose of extending federal powers.) One may say that the revisions were necessary, that the United States could not have prospered—perhaps even survived—without them, and that even if they could have been made by the amending process (which is doubtful), it was best that they were made without it because, as Publius said in *Federalist* 62, people feel some loss of attachment and reverence toward a political system when it is changed. But whatever judgments are made in these matters, there is no denying that the experience of the first fifty years supports the proposition that popular government cannot be relied upon to abide by the principles it has established itself upon.

The Wisdom and Virtue of the Politician

The leading nationalists held a common conception of popular government: that there existed a common interest of the society; that most men, if they recognized the common interest (which was unlikely), would, out of selfishness or other weakness, subordinate it to their special interests; that therefore, it was incumbent upon the wise and disinterested few to guide and direct the many, knowing that the cool and deliberate sense of the community, even if wrong, must ultimately prevail. This conception, on the basis of which the American government was formed and administered for half a century, was replaced by an altogether different one when John Quincy

Adams left the White House. Tocqueville, who came to America just then, found Americans devoted ("beyond reason") to the notion that man is endowed with an infinite capacity for improvement and committed also to the principle of self-interest rightly understood—the Americans' "chief security against themselves."[38] To the Founders (with the notable exception of Wilson), the notion of the goodness, let alone the perfectibility, of man was absurd: it was because men were not angels that government was necessary. As for self-interest, however understood, the Founders believed that if (as Tocqueville predicted) it became the sole spring of men's actions, it would be fatal to popular government. Republican government, Publius observed in *Federalist* 56, presupposes the existence of certain qualities—presumably wisdom and virtue—in a higher degree than any other form. Madison, writing while a member of the First Congress, described a type of government which he said did not exist on the west side of the Atlantic:

> A government operating by corrupt influence; substituting the motive of private interest in place of public duty; converting its pecuniary dispensations into bounties to favorites, or bribes to opponents; accommodating its measures to the avidity of a part of the nation instead of the benefit of the whole; in a word, enlisting an army of interested partisans, whose tongues, whose pens, whose intrigues, and whose active combinations, by supplying the terror of the sword, may support a real domination of the few, under an apparent liberty of the many.[39]

The changed conception of human nature implied that there was no need to enlarge the views of the ordinary man by passing them through the medium of a chosen body of citizens. And the legitimation of self-interest (whether rightly understood or not) produced the politician, whose function was to bring interests, however selfish, into the making of policy, in place of the statesman, whose function had been to discern the common good and lead men toward it. ("The race of American statesmen," Tocqueville wrote, "has evidently dwindled remarkably in the course of the last fifty years.")[40]

Political parties, which at first had represented opposed conceptions of the public interest, came more and more to represent private interests. ("America has had great parties, but has them no longer . . . ," Tocqueville remarked.)[41] For several decades, parties and politicians, especially those who saw national power as a threat to slavery, checked its growth. Lincoln, of course, asserted national power without limit; he violated the Constitution in order to preserve it.

11

Republican institutions were transformed into democratic ones. The electoral college remained, but presidential elections came to turn on the popular vote. In some states, senators were chosen de facto by straw ballot long before the passage in 1913 of the Seventeenth Amendment. The passage of the Sixteenth Amendment in that same year gave the federal government an ample revenue base and, incidentally, as George F. Break has observed, created a direct link between each taxpayer and Washington, one that invited "a whole new way of thinking about Washington's responsibility . . . ."[42] As more and more people left the relative security of the farm for the uncertainties of wage work in the cities, dependence upon government in times of distress grew.

Early in the New Deal the Supreme Court undid much of what remained of the Great Compromise by adopting Hamilton's interpretation of the "general welfare" clause. In *United States* v. *Butler* (297 U.S. 1, 66, 1936), in the course of finding the Agricultural Adjustment Act unconstitutional (as an invasion of the reserved rights of the states!), the Court declared that "the power of Congress to authorize expenditures of public moneys for public purposes is not limited by the direct grants of legislative power found in the Constitution." Later, in *Buckley* v. *Valeo* (U.S. 1, 424, 1976), it found that the power of Congress to provide for the general welfare extends to regulation of the financing of political campaigns.

It was not until after the New Deal that conditional grants became an important means of exercising federal influence. Beginning about 1960, the number of grant programs, as well as the number and stringency of the conditions attached to them, grew year by year until the states and cities depended upon the federal government for about one quarter of their revenue. Conditional grants do not give the federal government the veto power that Madison wanted for it, but their tendency, the editors of the *Yale Law Journal* have written, is to "allow the national government not merely to influence policy, but to make it." If federalism is to be taken seriously, they say, the states must have a zone of power belonging exclusively to them.[43]

Conclusion

I have tried to show that popular government has an inherent tendency to exceed whatever limits are constitutionally set upon its sphere. Insofar as men are free, they must be expected to use their freedom to renege upon agreements they deem contrary to the public interest or to their private interests. It is in the nature of politics that it cannot be confined to an agreed-upon arena.

The intention has not been to deplore the growth of federal power. It would be pointless to deplore what one maintains is inevitable. Apart from that, it is hard to believe that this nation could have prospered, or even survived, if—as Wilson assured the Pennsylvania ratifying convention would be the case—the congressional power had been collected "not from tacit implication, but from the positive grant expressed in the instrument of the union."[44] The state governments are well on the way to becoming mere administrative districts (what many of the Founders wanted them to become!), not very different from counties; that evolution may be regrettable, but it does not presage any calamity.

What *is* dismaying is the prospect that eventually—perhaps soon— the American people, having forgotten that the great principle of the revolution was limited government, will demand that government do what cannot be done, the attempting of which will destroy popular government itself.

Notes

1. For an account of early efforts to devolve federal programs, see Morton Grodzins, "Centralization and Decentralization in the American Federal System," in Robert A. Goldwin, ed., *A Nation of States* (Chicago: Rand McNally & Co., 1961), esp. pp. 4–15. For comprehensive treatment of a wide variety of issues relating to federalism, see the eleven volumes published by the Advisory Commission on Intergovernmental Relations under the series title *The Federal Role in the Federal System: The Dynamics of Growth*. The final volume was published in 1981.

2. The commission's recommendations appear in *Conference on the Future of Federalism: Report and Papers* (Washington, DC: ACIR, July 1981). The quoted words are on p. 132.

3. Herbert J. Storing, *What the Anti-Federalists Were For* (Chicago: University of Chicago Press, 1981), p. 53.

4. Hobbes wrote, "There must be some coercive power to compel men equally to the performance of their covenants, by the terror of some punishment, greater than the benefits they expect from the breach of their covenant." *Leviathan*, Part I, Ch. 15.

For Locke's formulation of the dilemma, see Robert Horwitz, "John Locke and the Preservation of Liberty," *The Political Science Reviewer* VI (Fall 1976), pp. 325–53. See also Robert A. Goldwin's discussion in his chapter on Locke in Leo Strauss and Joseph Cropsey, eds., *History of Political Philosophy*, (Chicago: University of Chicago Press, 1981), 2nd ed., esp. p. 473.

5. Max Farrand, ed., *The Records of the Federal Convention of 1787* (New Haven: Yale University Press, 1937), vol. III, p. 51.

6. Quoted by Gordon S. Wood, *The Creation of the American Republic, 1776–1787* (New York: W. W. Norton & Co., 1969), p. 467.

7. Charles F. Hobson, "The Negative on State Laws: James Madison, the Constitution, and the Crisis of Republican Government," *William and Mary Quarterly* 36, no. 2, Third Series (April 1979), p. 222.

8. Farrand, vol. I, pp. 27 and 51.

9. Ibid., vol. I, p. 24.

10. Ibid., vol. II, p. 27.

11. Ibid., vol. I, pp. 166–67.

12. *Federalist* No. 39.

13. Farrand, vol. III, p. 56.

14. Quoted by Hobson, pp. 230–31.

15. Farrand, vol. II, p. 10.

16. Ibid., vol. III, p. 56.

17. See James M. Buchanan "Ethical Rules, Expected Values, and Large Numbers," *Ethics* LXXXVI, no. 1 (October 1965), pp. 1–13, and Mancur Olson, *The Logic of Collective Action* (Cambridge, Mass.: Harvard University Press, 1965).

18. Farrand, vol. I, p. 135.

19. Gaillard Hunt, ed., *The Writings of James Madison* (New York: G. P. Putnams Sons, 1906), vol. VI, p. 70.

20. Farrand, vol. I, p. 406 and vol. II, p. 4.

21. Ibid., pp. 134–35.

22. Hobson, p. 231.

23. Farrand, vol. II, p. 28.

24. *Federalist* 55 and Hunt, vol. VI, p. 85.

25. Quoted by Alexander Landi, "Madison's Political Theory," in *The Political Science Reviewer* VI (Fall 1976), p. 87.

26. Farrand, vol. I, p. 60.

27. Ibid., vol. III, p. 254.

28. E. A. J. Johnson, *The Foundations of American Economic Freedom* (Minneapolis, Minn.: University of Minnesota Press, 1973), p. 260.

29. Merrill D. Peterson, ed., *The Portable Thomas Jefferson* (New York: Penguin Books), pp. 264 and 265.

30. Farrand, vol. II, pp. 321–22.

31. Jacob E. Cooke, ed., *The Reports of Alexander Hamilton* (New York: Harper Torchbooks, 1964), p. 88.

32. Ibid., p. 172.

33. Paul C. Peterson, "The Statesmanship of James Madison," in Ralph A. Rossum and Gary L. McDowell, eds., *The American Founding* (Port Washington, New York: Kennikat Press, 1981), p. 128.

34. Farrand, vol. III, p. 486.

35. Forrest McDonald, *E Pluribus Unum* (Indianapolis: Liberty Press, 1965), p. 306.

36. E. A. J. Johnson, p. 278.

37. Walter Berns, "The Meaning of the Tenth Amendment," in Robert A. Goldwin, ed., *A Nation of States* (Chicago: Rand McNally & Co., 1974), p. 148.

38. Alexis de Tocqueville, *Democracy in America* (New York: Alfred A. Knopf, 1948), vol. II, pp. 34 and 123.

39. Hunt, ed., vol. VI, p. 94.

40. Tocqueville, vol. I, p. 200.

41. Ibid., p. 175.

42. George F. Break, "Fiscal Federalism in the United States," in Advisory Commission for Intergovernmental Relations, *Conference on the Future of Federalism: Report and Papers*, p. 44.

43. "Taking Federalism Seriously: Limiting State Acceptance of National Grants," *Yale Law Journal* (June 1981), pp. 1695 and 1713.

44. Quoted by Storing, p. 63.

2

The Constitution: "A Firm National Government"

William Jeffrey, Jr.

To be clear about basic premises, let me say at the outset that the Constitution I shall be talking about is the Constitution as it came from the hands of its framers in 1787. This means that I shall have no concern with the accumulated mass of misconceptions, distortions, and misconstructions preserved for all time in the 400-plus volumes of the *United States Reports*. In adopting this viewpoint, I observe a distinction made by the late Frederic William Maitland between "the logic of evidence" and the "logic of authority."[1] For a number of reasons principally relating to legal education in this country, American lawyers are much too apt to believe that the meaning of the Constitution, or of any statute, depends completely on what some court has said about the meaning. As a matter of law—Maitland's term was "the logic of authority"—there is no denying the orthodoxy of this view. As a matter of history—"the logic of evidence"—this view is indefensible; from the historian's viewpoint, it is, almost of necessity, a process of perversion and misunderstanding.

The question, How federal is the Constitution? obviously involves the meaning of the Constitution, and, in accordance with the long-established rule of construction, our attention must be directed to the text of that document. It seems clear that the Constitution has meaning quite independently of what the Supreme Court has ever said about it. At least three of its framers, when they saw the final result, could not bring themselves to sign the document. They must therefore have been concerned with its meaning, and this meaning they understood without the benefit of any Supreme Court decisions. In addition, the people, or rather the special ratifying conventions, must have had some idea of the meaning of the document quite apart from anything the Supreme Court could have said about it. To adopt the contrary position seems to suggest that the three nonsigning framers and the special ratifying conventions were operating completely in the dark, in a mad whirl of noncomprehension and nonmeaning. I know of no basis for such an uncomplimentary view of the behavior of our fellow citizens in the eighteenth century.

Let me now state my response to the question, How federal is the Constitution? On the basis of the text of the document, I shall argue that no division of governmental powers between the nation and the states on any basis of equality is established, mandated, or implied by the Constitution.

Does the Constitution Require Federalism?

The first part of my discussion centers on those parts of the Constitution that have long been offered or interpreted as requiring what is called "federalism." In the main, there are three groups of such parts. The first is the extensive enumeration of congressional powers in Article I, section 8. The second consists of the provisions in Article III concerning the national judiciary and their supposed division of judicial power between state and nation. Last is the Tenth Amendment, added to the Constitution shortly after its ratification.

The view has long been entertained that congressional powers were enumerated in section 8 of Article I to grant the powers to Congress as against the states. The fact is that the powers were enumerated for three other, and very different, principal reasons.

The first of these reasons was to secure the powers to the Congress as against the executive, not as against the states. The standing law of 1787 as the framers knew it from Blackstone's *Commentaries* considered many powers "executive" that the framers did not wish the new American executive to have. Given the general language of Article II about the vesting of "the Executive power," explicit assignment of those powers to some other branch of the government was necessary. The framers' chosen depository for them was the two houses of the Congress of the United States.

The second principal reason for the enumeration stemmed from the drafting situation in which the framers found themselves. The Articles of Confederation, then in effect, contained in one form or another provisions about many of the powers dealt with. It was therefore simply prudent draftmanship to say something about them in the new Constitution, to cut off any possible controversy or any suggestion that, since the old articles gave the Congress the powers in question and the new Constitution made no provision about them, Congress would not have the powers under the new Constitution.

The third principal reason for the enumeration was somewhat

grammatical. The framers wished to limit the exercise of some of the powers of their new legislature, and some textual element was needed to which a clause stating the limitation could be attached.

An example will exhibit the combined operation of these factors. Congress has a power to establish inferior tribunals. In the first instance this is a grant of power as against the president, for under eighteenth-century views of the British royal prerogative, the power to create tribunals or courts was an attribute of the British monarch. To withdraw this power from the new executive, the framers had to assign it somewhere else; so they included it in the catalog of congressional powers. Second, the framers did not wish their new legislature to have an unlimited power to create tribunals. They therefore inserted the word "inferior" to qualify the word "Tribunals." Other provisions of the document are involved here. To anticipate very briefly: that adjective, "inferior," is included to fortify the constitutionally secured "supremacy" of the Supreme Court under Article III.

I turn now to Article III on the national judiciary, which supposedly divides the judicial power between the states and the national government. The particularly relevant clauses in this article are in the statement of the intended jurisdiction of the national judicial power. "The judicial Power," the document provides, "shall extend to all Cases, in Law and Equity, arising under this Constitution, the Laws of the United States, and Treaties made, or which shall be made, under their Authority."

The important thing about this clause is that it does not contain the word "statutory" before the word "laws," nor does it contain the phrase "made by the United States" after the word "laws." What I am arguing, therefore, is that the "laws of the United States" include the standing common law of 1787.

Support for this position is to be found in two things. Within the Constitution itself, this jurisdiction-granting clause may be usefully compared with the language of the supremacy clause in Article VI. In the supremacy clause, the phrase "which shall be made in Pursuance thereof" does follow the phrase "Laws of the United States." This wording very clearly restricts the status of supreme law to laws enacted by the Congress.

The highly significant fact is that such restrictive language was included in the initial draft of Article III of the Constitution as it came from the Constitutional Convention's Committee of Detail on August 6, 1787. Section 3 contained this language: "The jurisdiction of the Supreme Court shall extend to all cases arising under laws passed by the legislature of the United States." This wording would have established a clear limitation of the court's jurisdiction to cases arising under congressional statutes.

The convention reached its consideration of this language three weeks later, on August 27. On that date, as recorded by James Madison, John Rutledge of South Carolina moved that the words "passed by the legislature" be struck out; after the words "United States" the words "and Treaties made, or which shall be made, under their Authority" were inserted without objection.[2] If, then, the draft of the Committee of Detail explicitly limited the jurisdiction of the national judiciary to cases arising under "laws passed by the legislature of the United States" and the phrase "passed by the legislature" was struck out, the way is clearly opened to the inference that the common law of the country was admitted as an element in the mandatory jurisdiction of the national judiciary.

Despite the constantly reiterated talk of Madison and others of his party in later years, Article III on the national judiciary does not and cannot confer the status of supreme law on the common law of this country, because the common law was very carefully excluded from such status by the language of Article VI, in which the limitation to laws passed by the legislature was preserved.

As readers are aware, virtually no subject matter is not actually or potentially within the coverage of the common law. This very extensive jurisdiction of the national judiciary is not the only consequence of Article III properly read. The national judicial power includes other mandatory categories, the most important being the one that extends that power "to controversies . . . between citizens of different states."

Let me trace for you the intended, certainly the potential, operation of this mandatory category. In the framework that is nowadays known as the "diversity jurisdiction," assume that a case involving a purely common-law point in the law of torts has been decided between a litigant from Ohio and a litigant from Indiana. (Under the Constitution, this kind of case must be heard, sooner or later, by the Supreme Court of the United States, under the "all Cases, in Law or Equity" language.) What rule the Supreme Court may have laid down in deciding this diversity case is of no present concern. Furthermore, it could well have been decided as a "case of first impression," no English or American precedents being available. Nor is it in any way significant whether the plaintiff or the defendant has won. At all events, a precedent will now exist on the point of common law presented in the diversity case.

Next, assume that a case involving precisely the same point comes up between two litigants both of whom are from Indiana. According to perfectly natural lawyers' practice, one side or the other will wish to argue in a state court (if there are no federal courts) that the earlier Supreme Court precedent on the common-law point in the diversity

19

case is also a binding precedent in litigation on that point between litigants from the same state.

The final step in the example is clear. Under the slightly earlier provision of Article III that the judicial power "shall extend to all Cases in Law and Equity arising *under this Constitution,*" the unavoidable conclusion is that the question whether the diversity precedent is controlling in intrastate litigation is itself a question—a case in law and equity—arising under this Constitution. That means that the Supreme Court is given a power to vindicate its own precedents, a task that it will presumably discharge under the purpose stated in the Preamble of establishing justice throughout the country.

A related point requires brief attention. Since common-law decisions by the Supreme Court of the United States do not possess the status of supreme law the Congress is perfectly free to alter whatever rule of decision may come to be embodied in a line of Supreme Court decisions or even in a single case. This power, which so very badly frightened all Jeffersonians, comes from a part of the Constitution not yet scrutinized in this paper.

I refer, of course, to what has come to be known as the "necessary and proper" clause, the relevant language of which is as follows: "The Congress shall have Power . . . to make all Laws which shall be necessary and proper for carrying into Execution the foregoing Powers, and all other Powers vested by this Constitution in the Government of the United States, or in any Department or Officer thereof." One of the powers vested in the government of the United States is to "establish Justice," and the principal, though not the exclusive, means of establishing justice is the deciding of cases, a task obviously assigned to the national judiciary. Briefly, then, if the Supreme Court gets itself into a mess in the course of its intended decisional operations and can no longer distribute what in the opinion of the Congress is justice, the language of that clause gives Congress power to come to the aid of the national judiciary and help it carry into execution the powers vested by the Constitution in any department or officer of the government.

This is the rule-making power, and by now its terrifying feature will be apparent. Given the enormously broad scope of common-law questions, a congruent rule-making power was and will be coextensive with all possible objects of human legislation. Remember also that once the Congress enacts a statute anywhere within this immense field—and no part of the field is withdrawn from congressional power by the Constitution—that statute becomes, in the language of the supremacy clause, "the Supreme Law of the Land; and the Judges in every State shall be bound thereby, any thing in the Constitution or

Laws of any State to the Contrary notwithstanding."

I turn next to the portion of the Constitution that has probably been the most important element seeming to lend support to "federalism." The Tenth Amendment reads as follows: "The powers not delegated to the United States by the Constitution, nor prohibited by it to the States, are reserved to the States respectively, or to the people." From the language of the amendment, which speaks of powers not delegated, it is instantly apparent that some powers are indeed delegated and that only a consideration of those powers can determine what powers have not been delegated by the Constitution. The answer to the question what powers are delegated by the Constitution can, of course, only be answered by examining the language of the document, not omitting any of its language. In this connection consider the Preamble, with its very comprehensive series of six objects or purposes of government and six verbs:

> We, the People of the United States, in Order to form a more perfect Union, establish Justice, insure domestic Tranquility, provide for the common defence, promote the general Welfare, and secure the Blessings of Liberty to ourselves and our Posterity, do ordain and establish this Constitution for the United States of America.

The next step is to recur to the necessary and proper clause. The language there is that Congress shall have power to make all laws necessary and proper "for carrying into Execution . . . Powers vested . . . in the Government of the United States." The only point at which, within the four corners of the document, any powers are vested in "the Government of the United States" as distinguished from "any Department or Officer thereof" is the Preamble. Given the infinite scope of the six purposes with their six verbs, the resulting legislative power of Congress is likewise infinite (subject to any stated specific limitations). Thus once we are clear on the powers that are delegated by the Constitution, it is clear that virtually nothing is left that was not delegated and, in the language of the amendment, would therefore be reserved to the states or the people.

The next point is somewhat technical: the language of the Tenth Amendment speaks of "reserved" powers, not "retained" powers. The word "retained" was obviously known to the draftsmen of the amendment, for it appears in the Ninth Amendment, where the language speaks of rights "retained by the people." It is worth pointing out that in the two amendments the verb "retain" appears with "the people" but never with "the states."

The difference between the two verbs is best brought out by

considering the practice of conveyancers in real estate transactions. Assume a case where A is the owner of a tract of land. A sells half his tract to B but wishes to enjoy a right of passage over B's land. An easement will be created in the conveyance and is said to be "reserved" in favor of A. Should A later convey his part of the land—together with the easement in his favor—to C, the easement is said to be "retained" in favor of C. In the first transaction, then, the right was created for the first time.

The significant point is that the powers of the Tenth Amendment are *reserved* to the states; in other words, there can be no thought of antecedently existing powers in the states, which they "retain" under the amendment. The contrast with the language of the Ninth Amendment is striking, for there the people do "retain" the rights referred to.

Earlier I referred to the existence of the Articles of Confederation as constituting one element of the context within which the framers did their appointed work. Article II of the Articles of Confederation consisted of the following lethal language: "Each state retains its sovereignty, freedom, and independence, and every Power, Jurisdiction and right, which is not by this confederation expressly delegated to the United States, in Congress assembled."

What the framers did with respect to this article was to omit its language entirely from their new Constitution while including a great mass of other provisions. Whatever their reasons—and people will differ in their views about the cogency of the reasons—the framers also omitted a bill of rights, an omission that constitutes their most serious tactical error. The opponents of the document eagerly grasped this handle and, after a vigorous campaign of reiterated public mendacity that the liberties of America were in deadly peril, finally generated the first ten amendments to the Constitution.

The language of Madison when, on June 7, 1789, in the House of Representatives, he proposed what became those amendments is worth some attention.

> I find, from looking into the amendments proposed by the State conventions, that several are particularly anxious that it should be declared in the Constitution, that the powers not therein delegated should be reserved to the several states. Perhaps words which may define this more precisely than the whole of the instrument now does, may be considered as superfluous. I admit, they may be deemed unnecessary; but there can be no harm in making such a declaration, if gentlemen will allow that the fact is as stated. I am sure I understand it so, and do therefore propose it.[3]

In other words the gentleman who proposed what became the Tenth Amendment intended no change in the original system whatever, and he relied on the "whole" of the instrument.

I suggest that the vigorous opponents of the Constitution, those whose state offices had suffered a general cutting down to size, must have drawn but slight comfort from this amendment. Consider how much of the cherished Article II they did not retrieve: no "retaining" of any powers; and the grants under the new Constitution to Congress no longer had to be "expressly" delegated, that is, spelled out. Such, however, has been the advance of constitutional doctrine in this country that the Tenth Amendment has come to be viewed as a restatement of the old Article II of the Confederation. What a cruel trick to play on Mr. Madison!

Do Some Clauses of the Constitution Support Federalism?

I shall now deal with other provisions of the Constitution that, long overlooked or erroneously construed, have seemed to lend support to federalism. I believe I have sufficiently dealt with the first trio of clauses. I would remind readers of the total effect of the combination of the Preamble, the necessary and proper clause, and the supremacy clause as conclusive against any idea of apportionment of powers between the nation and the states.

I turn now to another clause that is generally not correctly understood today—especially the third important noun in its title. I refer to the time, place, and manner clause, which regulates the national electoral process. The language appears in section 4 of Article I, as follows: "The Times, Places and Manner of holding Elections for Senators and Representatives, shall be prescribed in each State by the Legislature thereof; but the Congress may at any time by Law make or alter such Regulations, except as to the Places of chusing Senators."

This clause exemplifies a device used by the Federal Convention at several points in the document: the Constitution specifies a procedure, a standard, or some provision and then grants to Congress a power to alter these arrangements if it wishes to do so. In this instance the power of prescribing "the Places of chusing Senators" is the single state power that is beyond the reach of congressional power under the original document. In other words, the framers did not want the Congress to have the power to prescribe to the states where their legislatures shall meet, for under the original document the choice of senators was confided to the state legislatures.

That tiny exception apart, all the remaining parts of the electoral process are confided to the states *in the first instance only*. People generally stop reading the clause at that point. The clause goes on,

23

however, to confer on the Congress broad discretion either to *make* these prescriptions, if a state has omitted to make them or to *alter* them if a state has enacted prescriptions that the Congress does not relish.

I have suggested that the third noun is the troublesome one, as far as the correct understanding of the clause is concerned. "Times" and "places" obviously present no difficulty, but what "manner" must mean—and it must if regulation either by states or by the Congress is to make any sense at all—is to prescribe who shall assemble as electors at the prescribed times and the prescribed places to do the voting. Obviously, the term "manner" concerns whether electors cast their votes orally or secretly or punch a button or place an X on a square, but these are incidental to the whole process. The essential matter is who does these things. If this scope of the noun "manner" is not recognized, there is no regulation of the electoral process. The conclusion is, then, that one area of legislative power long understood to be inviolably within the ambit of state power is, instead, subject to the virtually unlimited discretion of the national legislature.

The next clause to which I would draw readers' attention is the one known as the common defense and general welfare clause. This is in section 8 of Article I and reads as follows: "The Congress shall have Power To Lay and collect Taxes, Duties, Imposts and Excises, to pay the Debts and provide for the common Defence and general Welfare of the United States; but all Duties, Imposts and Excises shall be uniform throughout the United States."

This clause has generally been taken, under the Jeffersonian states' rights view, as prescribing the purposes of taxation—in other words, it is read as though the phrase "in order to" appeared before the words "pay the Debts." There is some undeniable force, I venture to the contrary, deriving from the ineluctable fact that the phrase "in order to" does *not* appear in the text of the document; so there is no textual compulsion to adopt the purposive meaning.

Assuming for the moment the purposive meaning of the clause, let me trace the logical and other snarls that appear under that mistaken view. The very next clause in the catalog of congressional powers is "to borrow Money on the credit of the United States." Readers will have no doubt whatever that borrowing money on the credit of the United States creates a debt of the United States, and under the previous clause Congress has the power to pay such debts. There is no limitation, purposive or other, on the congressional power "to borrow money on the credit of the United States." That is, Congress can borrow money whether or not such borrowing is conducive to providing for the common defense and the general welfare of the

United States. Thus to adopt the purposive meaning of the clause leads into inconsistency between these two powers of Congress.

Adopting the purposive meaning of the common defense and general welfare clause can also render some language redundant, and the orthodox rule at the time the Constitution was drawn and ratified—and still the rule today—is that any interpretation that requires discarding or ignoring language in the document being interpreted is *pro tanto* invalid. The argument will occur to some to import the limitations of the Preamble; in other words, money can be borrowed on the credit of the United States for the six preambular objects of the government. If this importing of limitations can be thus brought in, by parity of reasoning it can also be brought in with respect to the first power enumerated, "to pay the Debts and provide for the common Defence and general Welfare." That preambular language is already there, however, and the importation of language from the Preamble renders that already present language redundant. I know of no grounds for charging the framers or the entire convention (except the three nonsigners) with this kind of redundant draftsmanship.

The next clause to be examined comes from section 10 of Article I, the general catalog of explicit limitations on state power. The language runs as follows: "No State shall . . . pass any . . . law impairing the Obligation of Contracts." Under pressures too imperious to be resisted, this clause, fairly early—even during John Marshall's chief justiceship, with the chief justice not agreeing—was read as being limited to state impairment of contracts already formed. This view has gained some support from the equal prohibition against the state power to pass any ex post facto law, which was misconstrued as limited to criminal law only. This was not the understanding in the eighteenth century, when the Constitution was drawn, an ex post facto law being any statute, civil or criminal, that related to conduct before its enactment. If there is already a prohibition against ex post facto laws, the contracts clause, if it is to have any field for operation at all, must be prospective in its operation.

At this point a certain amount of legal metaphysics has crept in, the argument commonly being that the obligation of a contract cannot be impaired unless the contract is already in existence. Let me suggest a figure that may be helpful. There can be little question that the invention of the Model T by Henry Ford impaired the usefulness of horses, no matter whether the horses were alive on the day of invention or not. The usefulness of horses was impaired henceforth, including horses not yet born the day the first Model T rolled out of Henry Ford's shop.

Now, the obligation of any contract is the net result of a body of

25

laws and rules about contractual obligation in effect in a legal system. All readers have probably heard of the requirement in contract law of a consideration to support the obligation. Assume for the moment a legal system that does not have any such requirement. Assume further that a state legislature for the first time introduces this requirement for the making of binding contracts. I suggest that this legislative interposing of a further obstacle to the acquiring of contractual obligation "impairs" the obligation of contracts under that legal system. Conversely, were a state legislature to abolish an existing requirement of consideration for a binding contract, it would not impair, but would greatly enhance, the obligation of contracts. Such corrective action on the part of state legislatures remains a possibility, as far as the state legislatures' powers under the Constitution are concerned.

The last clause to be examined in this section is the imports and exports clause (section 10 of Article I):

> No State shall, without the Consent of the Congress, lay any Imposts or Duties on Imports or Exports, except what may be absolutely necessary for executing it's inspection Laws: and the net Produce of all Duties and Imposts, laid by any State on Imports or Exports, shall be for the Use of the Treasury of the United States; and all such Laws shall be subject to the Revision and Controul of the Congress.

The first detail on eighteenth-century word usage that is necessary to understand this clause is that imports and exports were not restricted to the nation's foreign trade. That restricted meaning did not become current in American constitutional doctrine until 1869, some considerable time after the convention in Philadelphia had adjourned sine die. The careful detail in this clause deserves particular attention. The framers begin with a nearly complete interdiction of such state legislative activity, by making it subject to the consent of the Congress; before a state even crosses the threshold, Congress must have said yes to the proposal.

Second, the states are not to make any revenue from their inspection laws, except what may be absolutely necessary for executing such laws—in other words, states can defray the costs of state inspection stations, inspectors' salaries, and necessary scales and other testing equipment. But no state is to make so much as a dime of revenue above and beyond those necessary expenses; the clause goes on to provide that should there be a net revenue from those inspection laws, it is to be held for the use of the Treasury of the United States. Just reflect for a moment, if you will, on the incalculable millions of dollars owed by the states to the Treasury of the United States—they could probably wipe out most of the national debt.

The framers were not done with this arrangement; although Congress must give its consent to state legislative activity under this plan, "all such Laws" that the states enact are to "be subject to the Revision and Controul of the Congress." In other words, Congress could entirely revoke its previously given consent and wipe out the whole nefarious scheme. I don't know whether any readers have ever been subject to the Balkanization of interstate travel in this country by having their cars searched for cigarettes or other "contraband" at some checkpoint on interstate highways, but a comprehensive remedy lies available to the Congress, whenever the politicians can summon up their courage.

The Context of the Framers' Language

Let us step back from the framers' language in the document and consider this closely related question: What were the circumstances, broadly viewed, in which this particular language came to be incorporated in the Constitution?

To begin at the most general level, I shall first look at the instructions given by the Continental Congress on February 21, 1787, to any convention that was to be assembled. These instructions are as follows:

> Resolved that in the opinion of Congress it is expedient that on the second Monday in May next a convention of delegates who shall have been appointed by the several states be held at Philadelphia for the sole and express purpose of revising the Articles of Confederation and reporting to Congress and the several legislatures such alterations and provisions therein as shall when agreed to in Congress and confirmed by the states render the federal Constitution adequate to the exigencies of government and the preservation of the Union.[4]

That resolution was preceded immediately by congressional language saying that "such convention appear[s] to be the most probable means of establishing in these states *a firm national government*" (emphasis supplied).

Note that the Federal Convention, to use language of James Wilson in that convention, was "free to *propose* anything" it wished.[5] It was not a plenipotentiary convention: whatever it came up with was to be reported to the Congress, agreed to by the Congress, and confirmed by the states. There is a fairly clear instruction: the convention is to report something that will establish in these states "a firm national government," not the "delicate federal system" of which so much has been heard in these latter days. Not only that, but the federal Constitution is to be rendered "adequate to the exigencies of government and the preservation of the Union."

The only verb that might give trouble is "revising" the Articles of Confederation. Notice, however, that nothing in the language of the congressional resolution calls for *preserving* any part of the Articles of Confederation. At any rate, the whole thing is subject to being reviewed or revised, so that the subsequent charges—some of them made during the convention—that the convention flagrantly disobeyed the Continental Congress's instructions are entirely groundless. Furthermore, any talk of a *coup d'état* in connection with the work of the convention is complete drivel. The delegates could not get away with anything in the draft they submitted as a result of their deliberations. The process of agreement by the Congress and confirmation by the states precluded any sudden overturning of anything. What were overturned were the delicate psyches of a great many state officials, and in view of their postrevolutionary performance, this could not have happened to a more deserving group of people.

The second example regarding the context in which the framers used the language they did concerns the commerce clause. The late William Crosskey has shown that the term "commerce" was used in the eighteenth century as a synonym for "all gainful economic activity" within the nation.[6] In other words, the commerce clause confides to the national legislature complete power, subject to limitations stated elsewhere in the document, to regulate the entire economic activity of the country. Despite the comprehensiveness of this grant of power, the clause has come to be understood as giving Congress power over only interstate commerce. The view that the clause is subject to that kind of limitation—false though it is—has fed, and has been fed by, the notion that there is some federal division of powers between the nation and the states.

The commercial powers of the national legislature under the Articles of Confederation, as everyone knows, were extremely defective. (The Congress, for example, had the power of "regulating the trade and managing all affairs with the Indians, not members of any of the states, provided that the legislative right of any state within its own limits be not infringed or violated.")

There was a business depression in the early and middle 1780s, a phenomenon not uncommon as a sequel to war. This depression was particularly severe in the New England states. In the spring of 1785 the merchants of Boston proposed to take action. They addressed petitions to the Massachusetts legislature. Acting in the well-established tradition of the committees of correspondence, the merchants' committee sent its resolutions in a series of circular letters to merchants in the seaports of the other states; they also sent copies to the Congress.

Their second letter, the one sent to seaports outside Massachusetts, includes the following paragraph containing the principal appeal of the letter:

> Persuaded, however, that the exertions of individual cities, or even states, without the support of the whole confederacy, will be inefficacious, or at most can operate only as a partial relief, and that nothing short of vesting Congress with full powers to regulate internal as well as the external commerce of all the states, can reach the mischiefs we complain of, we would agreeably to the directions of the enclosed proceedings, recommend to you an immediate application to the legislature of your state, to vest such powers in Congress (if they have not already done it) as shall be competent to the great and interesting purpose of placing the commerce of the United States upon the footing of perfect equality with every other nation; and to request you also to petition Congress (when they shall be thus cloathed with authority) to make such internal regulations as shall have that happy effect.[7]

Despite the extremely partial attendance at the Annapolis convention, which was called in response to this appeal, the commissioners in their report suggested that "the power of regulating trade is of . . . comprehensive extent." They went on to recommend that another convention be held in Philadelphia,

> to take into consideration the situation of the United States, to devise such further provisions as shall appear to them necessary to render the constitution of the Federal Government adequate to the exigencies of the Union; and to report such an act for that purpose to the United States in Congress assembled, as when agreed to, by them, and afterwards confirmed by the legislatures of every state, will effectually provide for the same.[8]

The commerce clause, or what was to become the commerce clause, first appeared in the Federal Convention in the report of the Committee of Detail, which the convention received on August 6, 1787. Under section 1 of Article VII, as it should have been numbered, the clause read "to regulate commerce with foreign nations, and among the several states." The convention came to the consideration of this article on August 16, and the clause in the report of the Committee of Detail was approved.[9]

On September 12 the Committee on Style reported, and in section 8 of their Article I this language appears: "To regulate commerce with foreign nations, among the several states, and with the Indian tribes."[10] In the closing days of the convention, some delegate or delegates perceived the omission of an important conjunction in the report of the Committee of Detail, and it was therefore moved to insert the word "and" after the word "nations."[11] This insertion makes it absolutely clear that there is no peculiar hybrid of commerce "with foreign nations" that might somehow happen to occur "among the several states"; instead, this is a separate and independent branch of the gainful economic activity of the American people that is being confided to the power of the Congress.

I have argued that the original Constitution does not establish, mandate, or imply any division whatever of governmental powers between the nation and the states. Fundamental to that argument is the further argument that the common defense and general welfare clause, which appears in section 8 of Article I, is properly construed as a separate substantive grant of legislative power, not as language merely expressive of the purposes of taxation.

In this connection, the reader must understand that the existence in the same section of an enumeration of powers of Congress does not wipe out the antecedent grant of general legislative power, nor does it reduce the grant to a mere synonym for the detailed catalog that follows, Madison's contrary argument notwithstanding. I have suggested that three principal reasons account for the appearance of the catalog of enumerated powers and that the enumeration would have been necessary for those three reasons whether or not the grant of a legislative power to provide for the common defense and general welfare appeared in section 8. Recall also that the common defense and the general welfare are included among the preambular objects of this government; the Congress of the United States, as the most democratically chosen branch of the national government, would be the proper repository for such vast powers.

I now put before the reader a brief account of the origin and growth of the general welfare clause in the proceedings of the Federal Convention. By way of preliminary, the reader should have some idea of the state of the surviving records of the Federal Convention. First, the official record, which was kept by Major William Jackson, secretary to the convention, is limited to recording the motions made and the actions taken on them by the convention, without any attempt to record the discussion on the floor.[12] The official publication of this *Journal* in 1819 was the initial breach in the wall of confidentiality that until then had stood around the convention's proceedings.

The inclusion of material from the floor debates is, of course, the great distinguishing feature of the famous notes made and preserved by Madison, the so-called Father of the Constitution.[13] Such has been the reiterated praise of Madison, however, that many people are likely to believe that in his famous notes we have a verbatim transcript of the convention's proceedings. Nothing could be further from the truth. Madison had the notes in his possession for almost fifty years; they were only published posthumously, in 1840, four years after his death, Madison being the last surviving member of the Federal Convention. There has never been any doubt that Madison "edited" his notes; the question is to what extent—and, I might add, for what purpose—he did the editing it is generally conceded that he did. Madison led an active political life in the decades after the convention and, not surprisingly for a politician, changed his views on a number of important matters during his lifetime. One rather unsympathetic fellow southerner remarked of Madison that he had been on every side of "every important question which had divided the public."[14]

Other members of the convention also made partial notes of its proceedings. Robert Yates, a delegate from New York, kept some notes, as did his fellow New York delegate, John Lansing, Jr., for that period of the convention when they were in attendance, before their departure in utter disgust at what they perceived to be the basic trend of the convention. Yates's notes, published in 1821, constituted the second block of materials on the proceedings of the convention to reach print.[15] Published during Madison's campaign for the presidency, the Yates notes are early in the series of incidents that stimulated Madison to "revise" his own notes, for, according to Yates's reports of Madison's speeches, Madison clearly appeared as espousing a considerably more nationalistic position than it had been and then was politically convenient for him to acknowledge.

The notes taken by Rufus King, delegate from Massachusetts, are of some importance in understanding the work of the convention, as another record made and preserved independently of Madison's. Other delegates—James McHenry of Maryland, William Pierce of Georgia, William Paterson of New Jersey—made notes of varying fullness, and Alexander Hamilton left a few brief memorandums, which throw more light on his position than on the thought and arguments of the other delegates to the convention.

We know from the diary of George Washington, who served as

elected chairman of the convention, that the convention sat "not less than five, for a large part of the time six, and sometimes seven hours a day, Sundays and the ten days adjournment to give the Committee of Detail a chance to prepare a draft excepted, for nearly four months."[16] Readers will recognize the pervasive incompleteness of the records of the convention when they learn that the notes for any one day collected from all the note takers just mentioned can easily be read through in two hours. The inference is that any venture into legislative history, such as that on which I am about to embark, must be limited to an account of the motions made and the votes taken on those motions.

After some necessary organizational measures, the convention got down to work on May 29, when Governor Edmund Randolph, head of the Virginia delegation, submitted a series of resolutions to serve as a starting point for its deliberations. Two of these resolutions deserve particular attention.

The first resolution was that "the Articles of Confederation ought to be so corrected and enlarged as to accomplish the objectives proposed by their institution; namely, common defense, security of liberty and general welfare."[17] This quoted some language of Article III of the Articles of Confederation, language that had appeared in the Franklin plan and in John Dickinson's draft of the articles.

The language of the sixth Virginia resolution runs as follows:

> Resolved, that each branch ought to possess the right of originating Acts; that the National Legislature ought to be impowered to enjoy the Legislative Rights vested in Congress by the Confederation and moreover to legislate in all cases to which the separate States are incompetent, or in which the harmony of the United States may be interrupted by the exercise of individual Legislation; to negative all laws passed by the several States, contravening in the opinion of the National Legislature the Articles of Union; and to call forth the force of the Union against any member of the Union failing to fulfill its duty under the Articles thereof.[18]

I think no one will argue that "the common defense" or "the general welfare," which cover almost all objectives of almost any human political society, are subject matters to which separate state legislatures could possibly be competent. On May 31 all of the sixth Virginia resolution but the last clause was approved by the convention.

On July 24 the Committee of Detail was chosen by the convention, the members being John Rutledge of South Carolina, Edmund Randolph of Virginia, Nathaniel Gorham of Massachusetts, Oliver Ellsworth of Connecticut, and James Wilson of Pennsylvania. Note the delicate balance on this crucial committee: two southerners, two northerners, and one from the middle states. By the time the convention's proceedings were referred to this committee, the resolution in question read as follows:

That the Legislature of the United States ought to possess the legislative Rights invested in Congress by the Confederation; and moreover to legislate in all Cases for the general Interests of the Union, and also in those Cases to which the States are separately incompetent, or in which the Harmony of the United States may be interrupted by the Exercise of individual Legislation.[19]

Mark the significance of the insertion in this latest version of that second branch of power, namely, "the right to legislate in all cases for the general interests of the Union," explicitly distinguished from those "cases to which the states are separately incompetent."

When the five-man Committee of Detail submitted its work to the convention on August 6, 1787, it was apparent to the convention, for reasons not now to be determined, that the committee had disobeyed its instructions and ignored the resolution I have been discussing. On August 22 Rutledge, chairman of the Committee of Detail, submitted to the convention a supplemental report from the committee. Among its provisions was one that proposed to add "at the end of the 16th clause of the second section of the seventh Article"

and to provide, as may become necessary, from time to time, for the well managing and security of the United States in such manner as shall not interfere with the Governments of individual States in matters which respect only their internal Police, or for which their individual authorities may be competent.[20]

The proposed change, which *restored* (conformably to the convention's earlier resolutions) the general legislative power "to provide . . . for the general interests and welfare of the United States," was now coupled with an internal-police limitation in favor of the states, all in explicit language.

The manner in which Madison in his famous notes handled the submission of this supplemental report is of singular interest. The text of the supplemental report, as printed in Farrand's *Records*, occupies about a page and a half. Even though Madison had, as long ago as 1789, written out his own copy of the *Journal* (now in the Yale University Library), the only thing in his notes is this cryptic entry:

"(here insert—the report from the journal of the convention of this date)."[21] This, of course, has the happy effect of forcing the readers of Madison's notes to go to a second record to get the language of the supplemental report. On the next page Madison reports as follows: "The report of the committee of five made by Mr. Rutledge, was taken up and then postponed that each member might furnish himself with a copy."[22] I would raise these two questions: Where was Madison's copy? And why didn't Madison include the text in his notes as finally left for publication?

On August 31 it was moved and seconded to refer such parts of the Constitution as had been postponed, and such parts of reports as had not been acted on, to a committee composed of a member from each state. This motion passed, and a committee was appointed by ballot, of Nicholas Gilman, Rufus King, Roger Sherman, David Brearley, Gouverneur Morris, John Dickinson, Daniel Carroll, Madison, Hugh Williamson, Pierce Butler, and Abraham Baldwin.[23]

This grand committee reported to the convention on September 4. The first clause of the first section of the seventh article was to read: "The legislature shall have power to lay and collect taxes, duties, imposts, and excises, to pay the debts and provide for the common defence and general welfare."[24] As readers will perceive, no instruction had been given to the committee to report any language regarding or defining the purposes of taxation. The phrase "in order to" is not in the text. On this day Major Jackson noted: "On the question to agree to the first clause of the report, it passed in the affirmative."[25] Madison says: "The (first) clause of the Report was agreed to nem. con."[26]

Readers will have noticed that the language in that supplemental report of August 22 providing for an internal-police limitation on the general welfare power of the national government was never approved by the convention, for no such limitation appears in the Constitution. This, of course, is the explanation for Madison's strange omission of the text of the report, to which I have referred. In other words, here was explicit language providing for precisely the kind of thing the states' rights party argued the Constitution meant, and the records of the convention show its explicit rejection.

On September 8 the proceedings of the convention as they then stood were referred to the Committee on Style, to which by ballot the convention had appointed William Samuel Johnson, a lawyer from Connecticut; Alexander Hamilton, a lawyer from New York; Gouverneur Morris, a Philadelphia lawyer; James Madison; and Rufus King, a lawyer from Boston.

This committee reported on September 12. Its report represents the moment in the convention's proceedings when the majestic language of the Preamble makes its initial appearance. Regrettably, perhaps, none of the working papers of the Committee on Style have survived. Of the five members not one was, at the time, anything but a firm nationalist. Merely on speculation, then, I suggest that the author of that preambular statement was Gouverneur Morris, who was so very obviously the floor manager of the nationalist party during the convention. Section 8 of Article I of their report now had in it the language that we have seen thus far and that has survived in the Constitution: "The Congress . . . shall have power (a) To lay and collect taxes, duties, imposts and excises; to pay the debts and provide for the common defence and general welfare of the United States."[27]

On September 14 the language "but all duties, imposts and excises shall be uniform throughout the United States" was added at the end of the first clause of section 8, Article I.[28] The sequence in which the various parts of this important clause came together, then, suggests the absence of any logically imperative connection between the power to lay and collect taxes, and so on, and the requirement that duties, imposts, and excises be uniform.

I have mentioned the three nonsigners of the Constitution, and at this point I want to put in evidence something of their views about the meaning of the document. On September 10 Randolph "took the opportunity to state his objections to the system." Among other points, he said his objections were based "on the want of a more definite boundary between the general and state legislatures—and between the general and state judiciaries."[29] Colonel George Mason, the second nonsigner from Virginia, was greatly upset by the absence of a declaration of rights. He thought also that the judiciary of the United States was so constructed and extended as to absorb and destroy the judiciaries of the several states.[30]

Conclusion

Finally, let me trail my coat through a few more fairs. By now, perhaps, most readers will be wondering how "general welfare" is defined. My answer is that the term can be defined only in the most general sense. As Madison once remarked in a letter, it is an inexhaustible fund of power; as James Bowdoin remarked during the ratification campaign, "the quantum of power cannot be estimated."[31] Briefly stated, however, the general welfare clause, always subject to the stated limitations elsewhere in the Constitution, confers on Congress the power to enact whatever measures a majority of the members in each branch of Congress feel will provide for the common defense or will promote the general welfare. (If the president disagrees, the Congress can override him by enacting its legislation with the prescribed special majority votes.)

I emphasize, however, that the reader should not overlook the specific limitations in the Constitution. For example, no matter how persuaded Congress might be that a three-year army appropriation act would conduce to the general welfare, it cannot, constitutionally, enact such a statute. Again, Congress may feel that a nonuniform naturalization law is just what the country needs; it cannot constitutionally, however, enact that kind of naturalization statute.

With more particular regard to the question of federalism, it may be useful to add a few words on the distribution of power established by the Constitution. In general, the state legislatures were continued in their preconstitutional amplitude of legislative power but with this extremely significant exception: they could no longer legislate in their accustomed sovereign-like fashion. Clearly, if the framers meant to terminate state legislative activity, they knew how to do so, and in section 10 of Article I they did it. That is the section that begins "No state, shall . . ."

In this sense, then, there was a kind of de facto federal system in the country after the adoption of the Constitution. States could go on, subject to whatever had been explicitly withdrawn from their competence, legislating as they had before; but henceforth Congress could occupy any given legislative field, and this continuing process would gradually reduce the scope of the states' legislative power.

From the foregoing, then, I draw this conclusion: we could have a federal system in this nation if the Congress wanted one. Federalism would then be the sequel to a conscious decision by the Congress that such a system would "promote the general welfare" of these United States.

Notes

1. Frederic W. Maitland, *Collected Papers*, ed. H. A. L. Fisher (Cambridge: Cambridge University Press, 1911), vol. 1, pp. 480–97.

2. Max Farrand, *The Records of the Federal Convention of 1787* (New Haven, Conn.: Yale University Press, 1966), vol. 2, p. 431.

3. *Annals of the Congress of the United States* (Washington, D.C., 1834), vol. 1, pp. 433, 441.

4. W. C. Ford et al., *Journals of the Continental Congress* (Washington, D.C., 1904–1937), vol. 32, pp. 73–74.

5. Farrand, *Records*, vol. 1, p. 253.

6. William W. Crosskey, *Politics and the Constitution in the History of the United States*, 2 vols. (Chicago: University of Chicago Press, Midway Reprint Series, 1978).

7. *Boston Gazette,* April 25, 1785.

8. Jonathan Elliott, *The Debates in the Several State Conventions on the Adoption of the Federal Constitution,* 2d ed. (Washington, D.C., 1936), vol. 1, pp. 117–18.

9. Farrand, *Records,* vol. 2, p. 308.

10. Ibid., p. 595.

11. Ibid., p. 610.

12. William Jackson, *Journal, Acts and Proceedings of the Convention, . . . Which Formed the Constitution of the United States* (Boston, 1819).

13. James Madison, *The Papers of James Madison,* ed. H. D. Gilpin (Washington, D.C.: Langtree and O'Sullivan, 1840).

14. James Madison, *The Writings of James Madison* (New York, 1900–1910), vol. 9, pp. 471, 473, 475.

15. Robert Yates, *Secret Proceedings and Debates of the Convention at Philadelphia, in the Year 1787, for the Purpose of Forming the Constitution of the United States of America* (Albany, 1821).

16. Farrand, *Records,* vol. 3, p. 81.

17. Ibid., vol. 1, p. 20.

18. Ibid., p. 21.

19. Ibid., vol. 2, pp. 131–32.

20. Ibid., p. 367.

21. Ibid., p. 375.

22. Ibid., p. 376.

23. Ibid., p. 481.

24. Ibid., p. 497.

25. Ibid., p. 495.

26. Ibid., p. 499.

27. Ibid., p. 594.

28. Ibid., p. 641.

29. Ibid., pp. 563–64.

30. Ibid., pp. 587–88.

31. *Documentary History of the Constitution of the United States of America* (Washington, D.C., 1894), vol. 5, pp. 334, 337–38.

3
Our Thoroughly Federal Constitution

Daniel J. Elazar

Contemporary Approaches

Since the late Martin Diamond brought the American academic and intellectual communities back to a concern with the political meaning of the Constitution of the United States of America (its full and proper title) and the founding of the American federal republic (whose regime he described as a democratic republic and which I describe as a federal democracy), the question of the federal character of the Constitution has been central to the discussion.[1] Diamond himself emphasized the importance of the federal dimension of the Constitution, and much of his writing focuses on it. Taking his definition of "federal" from late medieval sources and his interpretation of the Constitution from *The Federalist*, Diamond concluded that the federalism of the Constitution was constitutionalized decentralization rather than true federalism; the latter had been tried under the Articles of Confederation and had been found wanting. For Diamond, federalism—read constitutional decentralization—was an absolutely essential element of the American democratic republic. In that sense, he was a true friend of federalism.

While Diamond was formulating his argument, the late W. W. Crosskey was challenging the federal character of the Constitution in a different way.[2] His argument was a lawyer's argument, namely that the Constitution had to be read as a contract and when so read, with full understanding of eighteenth-century linguistic usage, it could only be understood as having established a modestly decentralized unitary state. Whereas Diamond's argument was political in the classic sense—his dispute with contemporary political science, for example, was over the political importance of institutions (including constitutions) and foundings—Crosskey's was utterly apolitical, as if, just because many of the delegates to the Philadelphia convention were trained as lawyers, they sat in the Pennsylvania State House and, as lawyers, negotiated a binding contract among several parties, which was to be unambiguous in language and inflexible in interpretation.

A different kind of intellectual assault on the fundamentally federal character of the Constitution came from political scientists of various kinds, who accepted the until recently unchallenged position that the Constitution was unambiguously federal, but who had concluded that federalism was obsolete or unjust or both. This is not the place to go into the intellectual history of their views. Suffice it to say that those views derived from two sources: (1) Jacobin-Marxian ideas that were embodied as political science jargon in the conception of the reified state, organized according to the center-periphery model, and (2) managerial theories that emerged in the twentieth century as part of the "scientific management" approach to the organization and direction of large organizations.[3] For some, these two sources combined to generate an unmitigated endorsement of centralization on all fronts: the presidency, constitutional law, government administration and finance, and the party system were to be centralized, on the grounds of both justice and efficiency. For others, all that was sought were organizational changes in the name of greater efficiency, whose consequences nonetheless were centralizing.

In the latter case, proposals for change endorsed federalism in principle even when undercutting it in practice. Perhaps the most extreme expression of the former view was William Riker's conclusion to his book, *Federalism*—namely, that to believe in federalism was to believe in racism.[4] In any case, the answer of those people to the question, How federal is the Constitution? would be: too federal for our times.

Since the presentation of these theories, the federal character of the Constitution has been reexamined by Vincent Ostrom, Martin Landau, and Heinz Eulau, among others, who have suggested that our founding document is not only quite federal, but properly so, in terms of political and administrative theory.[5] They not only see the federalism of the Constitution as a given, but they also understand it as a precursor of what today is known as cybernetic theory. Like their colleagues in political science, all are concerned in their analyses more with the results of the Constitution than with the intentions of the framers. In this respect, they differ radically from Diamond and Crosskey.

We can learn something from each of these approaches, even from those that are fundamentally wrong. But to answer the question, How federal is the Constitution? we must go beyond all of these views to examine (1) the intentions of the framers of the Constitution, of their constituents, and of those immediately responsible for translating the document into living reality; (2) the results that flowed from the Constitution; (3) the context in which the Constitution was conceived, drafted, ratified, and implemented; and (4) the ideas of those persons who did the work.

The Basis of the Argument

Several points must be made at the outset: (1) The Constitution was written by a committee; (2) it was written as a political document, not as a legal contract; (3) as such, its terminology reflects current fashion as well as precise usage and strives for ambiguity where it was deemed politically necessary to do so; (4) the framers of the Constitution drew upon more than one major source of ideas for their understanding of federalism; and (5) *The Federalist,* valuable as it is as a work of political thought and as an exposition of the Constitution, is not the whole commentary on the subject.

Contrary to the fashion—or to wishful thinking—among certain schools of constitutional interpretation, there is no "founder" in the American constitutional founding. The document was truly the product of a committee—perhaps the best committee ever assembled, but still a committee. Moreover, it was a broadly based committee, representing a wide range of views about the regime appropriate for the fledgling United States of America (a strong name applied to a relatively weak confederation of states). The convention committee included people as different as Alexander Hamilton, who wanted as strong a unitary state as he could get (his role as constitutional interpreter was more important than his role in the convention itself), and George Mason, who did not really want to change the Articles of Confederation in other than marginal ways. All the evidence points to a wide spectrum of views with regard to federalism, which converged both by necessity and inclination toward the honestly federal Connecticut compromise.

While the legal profession was nominally overrepresented in Philadelphia, it is common knowledge that legal training has been a major gateway to politics in American civil society, at least since the beginning of the eighteenth century. The men at Philadelphia were political leaders—politicians, if you will—above all else. They were engaged in the greatest of political exercises, the design and construction of a regime, and they were political artisans of the highest order. The business of the members of the Convention was the business of politics—the judicious mixture of fidelity to principle and felicitous compromise. Artful use of language is a major means of combining the two. Thus the language of the Constitution is crystal clear where possible and ambiguous where necessary, and the document must be read in that spirit. Nevertheless, until our own generation, one of the things of which there was no doubt was that the Constitution articulated a truly federal system of government. Even the opponents of its ratification—who held (as did Diamond 180 years later) that the term "federal" describes regimes we would call confederations to-day—never challenged the federal character of the new regime after the adoption of the Bill of Rights.

The federalism of the Constitution was crystal clear, just as the division and sharing of powers was left ambiguous. For men like Hamilton, the opportunities for centralization offered by the Constitution's ambiguity on the division of powers may have made the difference in their willingness to accept its federalism; and the same may have been true for those on the opposite side of the issue. Thus Americans were bequeathed what Woodrow Wilson later described as the "cardinal question of American politics." Crosskey's work is extraordinarily valuable in helping us understand eighteenth-century usages and, hence, what was made clear by the framers and what was left ambiguous, but I believe he is wrong to treat the Constitution as if it were a contract.[6]

Twentieth-century students of the Constitution who relied solely on *The Federalist* and certain anti-Federalist publications, have concluded that the framers of the Constitution were more or less exclusively products of classical education, of Hobbesian-Lockean political science, and of Enlightenment philosophy. No one would deny the existence of this "line of tradition" as a major factor in the founding of the United States of America, but there was another line of tradition actively represented in the founding as well: the Biblical-Reformed-Puritan tradition.

Both traditions address the idea and practice of federalism. The first tradition did, indeed, understand federalism as confederation—a strictly political affair, involving a permanent league of states in which sovereignty, indivisible by its nature, remained with the constituent units. The second tradition, however, came to federalism through theology—a theology known as federal theology, from *foedus*, or covenant, referring to the grounding of all human relationships in the original covenant between God and man described in the Bible and in subsequent subsidiary pacts. By the mid-eighteenth century, this tradition viewed federalism in theopolitical terms. Its federalism was not bound by classical notions of the polis, the perfectly complete polity that could at best be leagued with others; it functioned within

41

the Biblical framework of constituent polities held together by a shared common law and institutions—a concept much more like the federalism that emerged from the constitutional convention.[7]

The Biblical-Reformed-Puritan tradition of federalism was spread throughout British North America but, in particular, it took root and became the dominant tradition in New England. Connecticut was the first North American polity to be founded on fully federal principles— religious and political. It was literally a federation of four original towns, subsequently expanded. The constitution of that federation, the Fundamental Orders of Connecticut (1639), is a full statement of the tradition from its Biblical base onward. One hundred and fifty years after the founding of Connecticut, its sons, heirs to a long federalist tradition, proposed the Connecticut compromise and saved the Philadelphia convention.

In a paper prepared for the Workshop on Covenant and Politics of the Center for the Study of Federalism, Donald Lutz has demonstrated the power and ubiquity of this Biblical-Reformed-Puritan tradition in the process of the writing and adoption of the Constitution.[8] He, with his mentor Charles Hyneman, has explored all the known political writings of Americans in the era. As part of his analysis, he has enumerated the sources cited in connection with that process.[9] While *The Federalist* relies exclusively on classical sources, a point emphasized in others' analyses of the work,[10] overall, Lutz found that the Bible was the source most cited by far. Indeed, the book of Deuteronomy alone, with its discussion of the Mosaic constitution for Israel, is cited more than any other source.

Lutz's work (and that of students of eighteenth-century political history) throws different light on the subject, showing that we can no longer assume that the Constitution is solely a product of Locke and the Enlightenment. Perhaps if *The Federalist* had been written to persuade New Englanders or Scotch-Irish Presbyterians instead of already secularized New Yorkers, with their individualistic political culture, its authors might have turned to Biblical sources as part of their polemic.

That is why *The Federalist* cannot be considered the only authoritative commentary on the Constitution. Great as it is, its authors had more than one axe to grind. At the same time, others also wrote, preached, and argued the constitutional issues. Diamond, relying exclusively on *The Federalist*, could properly conclude that Publius pulled a sleight of hand in appropriating the term "federal" for the new Constitution, but for the people of Connecticut and the rest of the Calvinists in America, Publius was hardly changing definitions in midstream.

The Bicentennial of American Federalism

In 1776 the United States began the process that was to culminate twelve years later in the invention of modern federalism. In fact, the bicentennial of American independence in 1976 was also the bicentennial of American federalism. Since federalism is the *form* of American government that should not be surprising. (*Form* is used in its eighteenth-century meaning—the principle that informs the American polity in its every aspect.) The foundation of the United States was a federal act par excellence, involving a consistent and protracted interplay between the colonies-cum-states and the Continental-cum-United States Congress which the colonies created as a single national body to speak in their collective name.[11]

In the year that the representatives of the people of the colonies collectively declared the independence of the United States, other representatives of the same people were reconstituting the colonies themselves as states. Four colonies—New Hampshire, South Carolina, Virginia, and New Jersey—adopted state constitutions in 1776 before the adoption of the Declaration of Independence. Before the year was out, four more—Pennsylvania, Maryland, Delaware, and North Carolina—did likewise. Within sixteen months, all the former colonies except Massachusetts had adopted constitutions. Massachusetts wrote one but it took several years to be formally ratified by the voters.

In the interim, the Congress drafted the Articles of Confederation as a constitution for the United States (although it, too, was not fully ratified until 1781). At one time, this fact was used to argue that the creation of the states preceded that of the Union. Today it is generally agreed that they came into existence simultaneously—in the original federal act of the United States as such. In sum, all of the ambiguities of "diversity in unity" endemic to federalism were—fittingly—"present at the creation." Even local governments (in this case the towns and counties) got into the act as participants in the constitutional drafting and ratifying processes then, as now, not because they were asked but because they felt that they had as much right as any governments to do so.

In order to understand the more than two hundred years of American federalist experience, we must examine American federalism in the broadest sense of the term—not as intergovernmental relations, as federalism has come to be interpreted from the managerial perspectives of the twentieth century; not as a matter of the constitutional distribution of powers between the general and state governments, as constitutional lawyers are wont to see it; not even

43

as the grand political struggle between the Union and the states, which covered the canvas of nineteenth-century historians—but as something close to what the French term "integral federalism," that is to say, as the animating and informing principle of the American political system flowing from a covenantal approach to human relationships.

Let us begin at the beginning with the founding of the first British North American colonies. We must do so because American federalism begins at the beginning. Indeed, the development of the social, economic, and constitutional, as well as the political cultural foundations of federalism influenced the framers of the Constitution to invent the federal system for the new government. As in every other aspect of American life, the colonial background was crucial. It was within the five generations of American colonial history that the basis was laid for a covenantal federalism. It was laid so well that Americans have taken it utterly for granted and have virtually ignored it ever since.

The Four Roots of American Federalism

As the form of the American polity, federalism has its roots in the political, economic, social, and religious dimensions of American society. These several influences are often overlooked and have been especially neglected in our own time. The political roots of American federalism spring to mind most easily, the Articles of Confederation and the Constitution being the foremost examples. In fact, those roots go back at least to the Mayflower Compact, a federal document in the original meaning of the term—that is to say, a covenant among parties seeking to unite for common purposes while preserving their respective integrities. For all intents and purposes, the Mayflower Compact marked the first federal act on the part of people who were to become Americans. Between the Mayflower Compact and the Constitution of 1787 were uncounted compacts, covenants, and constitutions creating churches, towns, colonies, and at least one intercolonial confederation as well. Since we will have considerable occasion to examine the political behavioral roots of federalism in the following pages, suffice it to say at this point that those constitutional documents reflected as well as stimulated those behavioral patterns.

The economic roots of American federalism can be traced back to the early trading companies that sponsored British and Dutch settlement of North America and to the system of governance encountered by the settlers on the voyage over. The trading companies were royal monopolies organized on a shareholding basis, so that both ownership and control spread among the shareholders. In some cases, the shareholders remained in Europe and, on the basis of their control of the company, tried to hold the settlers within their grasp. This invariably failed, for political reasons. In a few cases, the settlers, or some significant portion of them, were themselves shareholders and as such combined political and economic control. In both cases, the pattern of shareholding led to a corporate structure that was at least quasi-federal in character.

The governance of ships had a contractual character that at least involved federal principles (in the original sense), whereby every member of a ship's crew was in some respects a partner in the voyage. By signing the ship's articles, a crew member was entitled to an appropriate share of the profits while at the same time submitting himself to the governance of the captain and the ship's officers. Thus every voyage was based on a prior compact among all participants, who determined the economic and political arrangements that would prevail for that voyage. This system resurfaced in slightly different form in the organization of the wagon trains that crossed the plains, whose members compacted to provide for their internal governance during the long trek to the Pacific.

The religious expression of federalism was brought to the United States through the federal theology of the Puritans, according to whom the world was organized through the covenants God had made with mankind; those covenants bound God and man into a lasting union and partnership to work for the redemption of the world, but in such a way that both sides were free (as partners must be) to preserve their respective integrities. This daring notion lies at the basis of all later perceptions of human freedom, since only free men can enter into covenants. Thus, implicit in the Puritan view was the understanding that God relinquished some of His own omnipotence to enable men to be free to compact with Him.

According to the federal theology, all social and political relationships are derived from the original covenant between God and man. Thus communities of believers were required to organize themselves by covenant into congregations, just as communities of citizens were required to organize themselves by covenant into towns. The entire structure of religious and political organization in New England was a reflection of this application of a theological principle to social and political life, and its echoes can be found in the economic life of the New England colonies as well.

Outside New England, perhaps half the churches and a fair share of the local governments as well were organized on the basis of congregational covenants. It has been demonstrated that early Virginia was also greatly influenced by Puritan ideas. Even after the eighteenth-century secularization of the covenant idea, the behavioral pattern persisted on every frontier, whether in the miners' camps of southwestern Missouri, central Colorado and the mother-lode country of California, or in the agricultural settlements of the upper Midwest.

It should not be surprising that the social dimension of federalism became so pronounced, given the convergence of these political, economic, and religious factors. Americans became socialized early into a kind of federalistic individualism—not the anarchic individualism of Latin countries, but an individualism that recognized the subtle bonds of partnership linking individuals even as they preserve their individual integrities. William James was to write about the federal character of these subtle bonds later in his prescription for a pluralistic universe.[12] Indeed, American pluralism is based on the tacit recognition of those bonds. Even though in the twentieth century the term pluralism has replaced all others in describing them, their federal character remains of utmost importance. At its best, American society becomes a web of individual and communal partnerships in which people join with one another to accomplish common purposes or to create a common environment, without falling into collectivism or allowing individualism to degenerate into anarchy. These links usually manifest themselves in the web of associations that we associate with modern society but that are particularly characteristic of covenanted societies such as the United States.

In a covenanted society the state itself is hardly more than an association writ large, endowed with exceptional powers, but still an association with limited means and ends. Were Americans, for some farfetched reason, to adopt a common salutation (like "comrade" in the Soviet Union or "citizen" from the days of the French Revolution), it would probably be "pardner"—the greeting of the archetypical American folk figure, the cowboy who embodies the combination of individualism and involvement in organized society and who expresses the character of that involvement through the term "pardner."

The Individual and Society: Contrasting Orientations

Implicit in the foregoing is a specific conception of the proper relationship between the individual and society. Perhaps more than any other polity in history, the United States has consciously and explicitly focused on that relationship as the cardinal question of politics. American history can be understood as a struggle among four major orientations to define the relationship between the individual and civil society (that slightly archaic early-modern term, conveying so well the political form of all comprehensive societies and the way good societies keep that political form from becoming all-embracingly totalitarian). All four orientations can be traced back to the first foundings of American settlements; they have continued to manifest themselves in the American experience ever since. One of the orientations is individualism. It is perhaps the best known and most celebrated—so much so that it is often thought to be the *only* legitimate American orientation. Another is collectivism, viewed by most as the opposite of individualism and as a kind of bogeyman to be rejected by all right-thinking Americans. A third is corporatism, an orientation rarely identified in its own right, yet a powerful influence on the course of American history. The fourth is federalism, a term as familiar to Americans as individualism, and in its own way almost as hallowed and certainly as misunderstood.

Americans and foreign observers alike have tended to emphasize American individualism. The American has been portrayed as the Lockean man, the solitary individual confronting a society that he has made through his contract with other solitary individuals, assessing both his rights and duties within the society on the basis of individual self-interest rightly understood. Society, in turn, confronts the individual in all its massiveness, uncushioned by mediating groups of other than transient character. At its best, America as an individualistic society emphasizes the importance of individual rights, the limitations those rights place upon governments, and the responsibility of government to preserve and protect those rights. At its worst, individualism has provided a cover for social irresponsibility, especially (but not exclusively) on the part of the rich and the powerful, and it has contributed to the sense of alienation on the part of the detached individual.

It was in answer to these ugly tendencies of American individualism that collectivism emerged as a major force on the American scene. Collectivist strains can be found from the very beginnings of American society. The first efforts at colonization on the part of the English, both at Jamestown and Plymouth, were based on collective effort and ownership. In both cases, within a year or two the experiment with collectivism was abandoned as a failure in favor of the encouragement of individual enterprise, with far better results. The collectivist strain periodically resurfaced in other colonization efforts, particularly in the utopian colonies of the nineteenth century. These experiments were the first attempts to use collectivism as an antidote to what were considered the evils of individualism and were initiated for the best of reasons. As long as the collectivist impulse was confined to a few relatively small experiments, and all of the colonies either disappeared or transformed themselves into noncollectivist communities, it had little influence on the body politic as such. Beginning with the New Deal, however, a collectivist approach began to be imposed on a national scale through massive government intervention.

The intellectual origins of this collectivist approach can be found in the post–Civil War years—more specifically, in the last generation of the nineteenth century—when intellectual reformers, seeking to eliminate the evils of industrial society while retaining the benefits of industrialization, began to propose collectivist solutions to current social problems. Perhaps the foremost example of this new collectivist utopia was provided by Edward Bellamy in his novel, *Looking Backward*,[13] In it he describes a society organized on military principles, in which every person is mobilized for the active adult portion of his or her life, within one grand pyramid, to undertake the tasks of society. At the time, Bellamy's utopia was widely admired, and clubs were established all over the country to advance his scheme. Today, with the experience of such utopias in other parts of the world vividly before us, we are appropriately horrified by the collectivist regimentation and appalled at Bellamy's naiveté regarding human nature and the exercise of power.

Less radical expressions of this collectivist impulse are to be found in the writings of individuals like Herbert Croly, often identified with the Progressive movement.[14] Croly's ideas had a substantial influence because he did not seek an utter transformation of American society, but rather an amelioration of existing conditions through more national government effort on a collectivist basis. The Crolyan image provided the basis for the kind of collectivism that emerged during the New Deal.

This is not to say that the New Deal was itself collectivist. It was far too unsystematic for that, and it is unlikely that Franklin D. Roosevelt wished to foster a collectivist America; but some of those around him saw in collectivism—democratic collectivism to be sure—the only solution to the problems facing the country. In the intervening decades, they and their heirs have cultivated a substantial collectivism within the body politic by capitalizing on the moralistic strain in American society, which periodically encourages Americans to impose uniform standards of behavior, even in delicate areas, upon the American public. Needless to say, the result is not known as collectivism. Sinclair Lewis once said that fascism could come to the United States only in the name of liberty. So, too, with collectivism.

Collectivism American-style has been reinforced by a third strain in American life: corporatism. In this context, corporatism may be defined as the organization of civil society through corporate structures that are able efficiently to focus considerable power and energy on the achievement of specific goals and that tend to combine with one another to control common fields of endeavor. Those fields are primarily economic, but may be political as well. Such corporate bodies, while nominally broad based, are in fact excellent devices for concentrating control in the hands of managers who are formally trustees for the broad group of owners (shareholders), but who in fact have great freedom to maneuver. In return for relinguishing control to managers through the corporate framework, the shareholders are in a position to profit without sharing responsibility, since the corporation becomes a reified person standing apart from those who have combined to form, own, and manage it.

It is easy to see how corporatism of this kind can be linked closely with a kind of collectivism. In fact, that link also began with the first English settlements on American shores. The first settlers were sent out by the great trading companies of England and Holland, the predecessors of modern corporations. Those trading companies used collectivist mechanisms to build their colonies until the mechanisms proved unprofitable. This phase of corporatism did not last much beyond the first generation of settlement in each of the colonies. The settling of the original colonies through such corporate structures, however, has a significance that often has been overlooked in American history: only after corporate endeavors had laid the groundwork could other settlement agencies pick up the momentum.

Much the same pattern recurred at each successive take-off point in the advance of the land frontier. Thus, settlement of the trans-Appalachian West owed much to the initial work of fur and land corporations, while subsequent settlement of the trans-Mississippi West was initiated in no small measure by larger fur corporations and the great railroad corporations. The urban-industrial and metropolitan-technological frontiers are closely related to corporatism. The initial wave of entrepreneurs on the urban-industrial frontier organized corporate structures. Indeed, the struggle in the Jacksonian era over the freedom to incorporate was crucial to the opening and development of that frontier. By the time of the opening of the metropolitan-technological frontier, pioneering itself was a corporate activity, in a manner reminiscent of, but even surpassing, the earliest days of land settlement.

In the era of the land frontier, corporatism had strong competitors, so its role remained significant but not dominant, resurfacing at key junctures in American development, but then having to retreat before other factors. Even the nascent corporations were subject to other strong influences, so that corporatism, as such, had less of an impact. Only on the urban-industrial frontier did corporatism play a major role, but it was still by no means a dominant one. Corporations assumed significant economic roles and involved themselves in politics as a result, primarily to protect and advance their own interests. Even the most ruthless among them, however, did not seek to provide a model for organizing the polity. It was understood that corporate and political organizations existed for different purposes and hence drew from different models. Nonetheless, intellectual reformers in the last generation of the nineteenth century based many of their reform proposals on corporate models. They were joined in the Progressive Era by spokesmen for corporate interests, who saw in the smooth workings of the great business corporations models to be adopted by government—particularly by municipal government—to improve their efficiency.

Still, it was only with the coming of the metropolitan-technological frontier in the generation following World War II that the political realm equated the corporate model with progress. In that generation, there was a movement toward linking corporatism and collectivism. This in itself was a revolutionary shift. Collectivism originally was fostered in government to fight corporate power. In the end, however, the natural affinity of the two brought them together, at the expense of individualism and federalism.

The American people, priding themselves on their individualism are, for the most part, unaware of the role corporatism has played in their history, even though they have adopted many of its basic assumptions. Thus, for example, since Americans have defined efficiency in commercial terms (that is to say, what is efficient for the promotion of commerce is accepted as efficient for all purposes), they increasingly have come to accept corporate definitions of efficiency, as corporations have become the dominant forces in commerce. Political life has thus been pushed in the direction of corporatist ideas, with few asking whether the basic assumptions of corporatism are applicable or appropriate in a democratic political arena.

Federalism is the fourth orientation in American life; it has so dominated the American experiment that it has been taken utterly for granted. Since the days of the Puritan and Revolutionary Founders, when John Winthrop could still talk of federal liberty and Thomas Jefferson of ward republics, federalism has sunk deeply into the American psyche. Only in civil societies where some people are searching for the federalist way—in France, for example—is federalism identified as a sociopolitical orientation in its own right. Intellectuals in those countries write about "integral federalism." In the United States, federalism has been so integral to the American experience, that there has been no incentive to discuss integral federalism as a concept.

Federalism as an orientation emphasizes each individual's place in a network of cooperative communities, where individualism is defined not through one's detachment but through partnership with others—a network in which the individual does not confront society alone, but through such mediating institutions as the family, the religious community, an ethnic group, or the like. The federalist way has limited the anarchic tendencies of individualism, and has generated the kind of disciplined independence that has characterized American society. The federalist way has enabled Americans to undertake collective action without embracing collectivism. Finally, the federalist way has provided both the political and social dimensions necessary to harness the power generated by corporatism and to direct it toward the goals of justice that animate American civil society.

The Origins of American Federalism

As the literature of the constitutional ratification campaign (both Federalist and Anti-Federalist) indicates, federalism was designed by the Founding Fathers to be more than a structural compromise, to make possible the unification of the several states under a single national government. It was also to be more than an expedient geographic division of power. Federalism represented to its American creators a new political alternative for solving the problems of governing civil societies, an alternative that embraced the panoply of political theories, institutions, and patterns of behavior that must be harmonized in order to form a political system.

The federalism of the Founders was designed to provide an enduring framework of government, a successful system of politics, a reasonable approach to the problems of popular government, and a decent means for securing civil justice and morality. Its inventors conceived of federalism as a way to solve the perennial problems of any civil society: the problems of balancing human liberty, political authority, and governmental energy to create a political system at once strong, lasting, democratic, and just. They believed their invention could solve those problems because it was based on valid fundamental principles and it employed appropriate, if new, political techniques to effectuate (at least approximately) those principles. They were convinced of this—and were soon joined in their conviction by the American people—because their invention directly resolved important substantive questions that, they anticipated, would confront the United States. The essence of their solution was the application of the federal principle not only to relations between governments but also to the overall political relationships of groups ("factions," in Madison's terminology) and of individuals, to government.

The records of the founding contain the arguments that make clear to us why the Founders felt as they did. Unfortunately, current myths prevent many from considering those sources on their own terms. For one thing, there are too many who believe American federalism is the product of circumstances alone—that nature itself (or at least prior experience) dictated that the American republic be built on the rock of diffused governmental powers. According to this view, any discussion of a "federal principle" is merely an ex post facto attempt to discover a unique or original political concept, when common political considerations actually suffice to explain it. Pointing to the vast expanse of land under the American flag even in 1787, the great diversity of peoples gathered under its protection, the general commitment to popular government throughout the land, and the preexistence of the thirteen colonies, many people conclude that a formal distribution of power among "central" and "local" governments was inevitable if there were to be any union at all; the Founders of the republic simply worked out the mechanisms needed to make the status quo politically viable.

This view has been widely accepted in the twentieth century because it appeals to those who subscribe to two other contemporary views of American federalism. One is the view that the framers of the Constitution were hostile to popular government and used federalism to limit "democracy" by distributing powers undemocratically. This school understands subsequent American history as the struggle to establish popular government against the spirit of the Founders' Constitution. Accordingly, they believe that the Constitution's provisions for the distribution of power become increasingly obsolete as the nation becomes more "democratic." The other view also accepts the premise that the Founders were antidemocratic, but it "excuses" them on the grounds that problems of communication over such a vast and diverse area at the time required the federal distribution of powers. Their argument is that as communications become faster and easier, the federal distribution of powers becomes obsolete.

At first glance, history appears to support the current myths. The implantation of settlements on the American shores under different regimes and charters had led to the emergence of at least thirteen firmly rooted colonies-cum-states by 1776. The new nation did inherit the basis for some type of federal plan and, it might even be said, had no choice in the matter. Recent research has heightened the plausibility of this view by revealing the extent to which the American colonies enjoyed a de facto federal relationship with the English king and Parliament before achieving independence.

The existence of states, however, was no guarantee that they could be united under one government. Moreover, there was no guarantee that unification could take any form other than loose confederation as long as the states remained intact as sovereign civil societies or any form other than consolidation if they did not. The factors of size and diversity were not determinative. Distribution, as opposed to concentration, of power is not a function of size and diversity per se, but a function of republican political inclinations.

Students of comparative government—from the days of Aristotle to our own, and including the generation of the Founders of the republic—have been fully aware of the possibilities for centralized government in even the largest and most diverse empires. In Aristotle's day the Persian Empire extended for over three thousand miles, "from India to Ethiopia," and included over a hundred different nationality and ethnic groups, each located in its own land; yet throughout its two hundred years of existence, it was governed by a despotism which, while maintaining a benevolent attitude toward the maintenance of local customs and civil laws, concentrated as much political power as possible in the hands of the emperor.

Locke, Montesquieu, and the Founding Fathers were acquainted with the similarly organized Ottoman Empire. They, like our own generation, also encountered one of the greatest centralized despotisms of all time, in the form of the Russian Empire. When Cortez was viceroy in Mexico, the Russian Empire under Ivan the Terrible already covered an area larger than the original United States (888,811 square miles in 1789). The Russians began their march eastward in the sixteenth century and reached the Pacific at the time the Puritans were settling in New England. By the year of the Glorious Revolution and the establishment of parliamentary supremacy in England, the Russians had consolidated their centralized rule over some seven million square miles and dozens of nations, peoples, and tribes. An eighteenth-century Russian, if asked about the political consequences of a large domain, would have been likely to say that a great expanse of territory is useful in protecting absolute rule, since the difficulties of internal communication created thereby help prevent popular uprisings on a nationwide scale.

A Frenchman of the same century, if asked the best method of creating a nation out of a number of smaller "sovereignties," would undoubtedly have recalled the history of France and advocated the complete political and administrative subordination of the entities to a central government and the elimination of all vestiges of local autonomy in order to minimize the possibilities of civil war. Even an eighteenth-century Englishman, aware of the centuries-old problem of absorbing Scotland within Great Britain, would probably have approached the problem of national unification similarly, except that he might have added a touch of decentralization as a palliative. Thinking Americans were aware of all these examples in 1787. It is no accident that *The Federalist* had to concentrate heavily on refuting the argument that a stronger national government would inevitably open the door to centralized depotism.[15]

Closer examination of the situation between 1775 and 1801 provides convincing evidence that—regardless of the factors that might encourage some division of power between national government and the state governments—the development of a federal system stronger than that embodied in the Articles of Confederation was not foreordained. Such an examination also reveals the level of commitment of the Founders to the idea of popular government and to the search for the best form of organization—the best constitution—for the republic, one that would secure the liberties of the people while avoiding the weaknesses of past experiments in popular government.

Even here, the Founders had little precedent to guide them. Not only were there no extant examples of the successful governance of a *large* territory except through a strong centralized government, but there were few *small* territories governed in a "republican" manner, and none offered the example of federalism as Americans later came to know it. The two nations then existing that had come closest to resolving the problems of national unity without governmental centralization were the United Provinces of the Netherlands and the Swiss Confederation. Both, however, were very small republics (each covered about 15,000 square miles at that time); furthermore, the failure of the Netherlands to solve its constitutional problems and its consequent lapse into government by an incompetent executive and an antirepublican oligarchy were well known, while the Swiss Confederation was hardly more than a protective association of independent states with little national consciousness. Neither could be an attractive example to the American nation builders, who were committed both to republicanism and to the common nationality of all Americans.

The Founding Fathers could have attempted to bring the several states together into a single unified but decentralized state on the order of the government of Great Britain; or, they could have been satisfied with a loose confederation of sovereign states, united only for purposes of defense and foreign relations and, while barely able to govern adequately even in the areas of its responsibility, at least offering minimal opportunities for national despotism.

There were those who advocated the former course, particularly among the younger officers of the Continental Army. At various times, they urged Washington to establish a constitutional dictatorship (which possibly could have led to a political system akin to the totalitarian democracy established by Napoleon in France in the 1790s), or to assume the crown as a constitutional monarch (which presumably would have led to a political system akin to the aristocratic oligarchy that existed in eighteenth-century England). Although Washington effectively subdued most of them on several occasions during the war itself (the most famous of which was his farewell at Fraunces Tavern), one of their number, former lieutenant-colonel Alexander Hamilton, continued to advocate the latter position as much as he dared right through the Constitutional Convention.

The second course was the one followed during the war as a natural outgrowth of the Continental Congresses assembled from 1765 through 1775. If the Founders had been content with a "foreordained" system, one "dictated" by the actual status of the United States in 1776, they would have accepted this alternative and retained the Articles of Confederation that were adopted to ratify just such a confederacy. That system has been compared most frequently to the various Hellenic leagues, which united several city-states only in regard to a limited common purpose—invariably that of defense. Such leagues often embraced small despotisms as well as small democracies. They had little or no role to play in determining the internal regimes of member states and were in no sense protectors of human liberties or popular government.

Among those who advocated this course of action were some of the most notable patriots of the early Revolutionary struggle. Above all, they feared despotism in large governments and distrusted any notion that a national government with energy could be kept republican. Whatever their views as to the potential tyranny of the majority, they were more willing to trust smaller governments with supervision of the people's liberties on the grounds that they were more accessible to the people. Patrick Henry was the most outspoken of this group. He held his ground to the bitter end, uncompromising in his belief.

Popular Government and the Federal Solution

As we all know, the Founders chose neither course, but invented a third one of their own. Their choice was animated by a desire to perfect the union of what they believed to be an already existing

55

nation, to give it the power to act as a government while keeping it republican and democratic. In developing their solution, they transcended the limits of earlier political thought in order to devise a way to protect the people's liberties from every threat.

Their alternative reflected a great step forward in thinking about popular government, because they refused to accept the simplistic notion that the likelihood of despotism increased in direct proportion to the size of the country to be governed. They were fully convinced by history and personal experience that small governments—in their case, the states—could be as despotic as large ones.

Moreover, the Founders were convinced by history and experience that democratic governments could be as as tyrannical as autocratic ones, if they were based on simple and untrammeled majoritarianism. Pure democracies, in particular, were subject to the sway of passion and hence to the promotion of injustice, and even republics were susceptible, if factions were allowed to reign unchecked. As friends of human liberty and popular government, they felt it necessary to create a political system that would protect the people from despotic governments, whether they be large or small, democratic or not.

Their solution was federalism. It was designed to balance all contingencies, thereby creating permanent points of tension that would limit the spread of either popular passion or governmental excess, break up or weaken the power of factions, and require broad-based majorities in order to take significant political actions. To the Founders, locating all sovereignty in the people as a whole, while dividing the exercise of sovereign powers among several governments—one general, the others regional—was a means of checking despotic tendencies, majoritarian or otherwise, in both the larger and smaller governments, while preserving the principle of popular government. The interdependence of the national and state governments would ensure their ability to check one another and yet enable them to cooperate and govern energetically. In the words of Publius, the Founders advocated "a republican remedy for republican diseases."

In organizational terms, the perennial tug of war between centralization and decentralization was to be avoided by the introduction of the principle of noncentralization. The difference is a crucial one. Decentralization, even as it implies local control, assumes the existence of a central authority with the power to concentrate, devolve, or reconcentrate power more or less at will. Noncentralization assumes that there is no central authority as such, that power is granted directly by the people to several national and regional authorities and, even though the national authority may enjoy an ultimate preeminence, that those authorities cannot legitimately take basic power away from each other.

True federal systems must be noncentralized systems. Even when, in practical situations, there seems to be only the thin line of the spirit between noncentralization and decentralization, that thin line determines the extent and character of the diffusion of power in a particular regime.

The American people and their leaders were to extend this aspect of federalism—partially described in common parlance as the system of checks and balances—into most other areas of their political life. Both the state governments and the national government have powers that neither take from the other, even when both share in their exercise. This principle had been applied earlier to relations between the various branches of government—executive, legislative, and judicial—even before the invention of federalism. It was subsequently applied to the structure and organization of the party system, which consists of two national coalitions of substantially independent state and local party organizations, each further checked by the independence of action reserved to the "congressional parties" within the two coalitions. It was applied to other processes of politics, and even to the nation's economic system, in ways too numerous to mention here.

The federal principle sets the tone for American civil society, making it a society of balanced interests with egalitarian overtones, just as the monarchist principle makes British civil society class- and elite-oriented despite democratic pressures, and just as the collectivist principle sets the tone for Russian civil society, making it anti-individualistic even where equalitarian. In political terms, the federal principle establishes the basic power distribution within American civil society. The Founders understood the role of such central principles in setting the framework for the development of a political system. They knew that, while the roots of the central principle of every civil society are embedded in its culture, constitution makers do have a significant opportunity to sharpen the principle's application and the direction of its future growth.

In sum, federalism as the Founders conceived it was an effort to protect the rights of men by consciously creating institutions and procedures that would give government adequate powers and at the same time force the governors to achieve general consent from all segments of the public before acting in other than routine ways. Requiring extraordinary majorities for great actions, the Constitution was based on the idea that there is a qualitative difference between a simple majority formed for a specific issue and the larger consensus that allows governments to function continuously from generation to generation.

The Covenant Idea and the Federal Principle

The American federal system was, at the same time, both a new political invention and a reasonable extension of an old political principle—a considerable change in the American status quo, and a step fully consonant with the particular political genius of the American people. Partly because of their experience with the model before them and partly because of the theoretical principles they had derived from the philosophic traditions surrounding them, the American people rejected the notions of the general will and the organic state common among their European contemporaries. Instead, they built their constitutions and institutions on the *covenant* principle, a very different conception of the political order and the one most conducive to the theory and practice of federalism.

This notion of covenant—of a lasting yet limited agreement between free men or between free families of men, entered into freely by the parties concerned to achieve common ends or to protect common rights—has its roots in the Hebrew Bible. There the covenant principle stands at the very center of the relationship between man and God and also forms the basis for the establishment of the holy commonwealth. The covenant idea passed into early Christianity only after losing its political implications. Its political sense was restored during the Protestant Reformation, particularly by the Protestant groups influenced by Calvin and the Hebrew Bible, the same groups that dominated the political revolutionary movements in Britain and America in the seventeenth and eighteenth centuries. Much of the American reliance upon the covenant principle stems from the attempts of religiously inspired settlers on these shores to reproduce that kind of covenant in the New World and to build their commonwealths upon it. The Yankees of New England, the Scotch-Irish of the mountains and Piedmont from Pennsylvania to Georgia, the Dutch of New York, the Presbyterians, the Jews, and, to a lesser extent, the Quakers and German sectarians of Pennsylvania and the Middle States were all nurtured in churches constructed on the covenant principle and subscribing to the federal theology as the means for delineating properly (according to the scheme revealed by the Bible itself) the relationship between man and God, and, by extension, between man and man.

By the middle of the eighteenth century, however, the covenant idea had been severed from its religious roots and secularized by men like Hobbes, Locke, and Rousseau. They transformed it into the concept of the *political compact*, the freely assumed bond between man and man that lifted them out of an unbearable state of nature and into civilization. In the Lockean view widely admired by Americans, it was this political compact that made popular government possible. The availability of the covenant idea in two forms meant that those Americans who did not acknowledge the political character of the covenant between man and God inevitably recognized the political character of the compact between man and man and built their constitutions upon that.

The evidence is overwhelming that the covenant principle, carried into the larger political realm as part of the development of modern popular government, became the foundation for the idea of federalism. The history and meaning of the term itself reveals this. The word federal was first used in 1645 during the English civil war to describe covenantal relationships of both a political and a theological nature. Apparently, as its theological usage would indicate, the term implied a closer or more permanent relationship than its slightly older companion, *confederal*, a middle English derivative of the same Latin root. At first the two words were so closely related that they were used synonymously; the American Civil War, however, added a dimension to the theory of federalism by sharpening the distinction between them. *Federal* was not used in its present sense until 1777 during the American Revolution. Its modern usage, then, is an American invention. The creation of the term *federalism* to indicate the existence of a "federal principle or system of political organization" (quoting the Oxford Universal Dictionary), did not come until 1793, after the principle was already embodied in a great work of political theory and in the constitution of a potentially great nation.[16]

Covenant (or federal) theory was widely appreciated and deeply rooted in the American tradition in 1787 because it was not the property of philosophers, theologians, or intellectuals alone. In its various adaptations, it was used for a number of very public enterprises, from the establishment of colonial self-government to the creation of the great trading corporations of the seventeenth century. Americans made covenants or compacts to establish new civil societies regularly. Witness the Mayflower Compact (1620):

> In the name of God, Amen. We whose names are under written . . ., Having undertaken for the Glory of God, and Advancement of the Christian Faith, and the Honour of Our King and Country, a Voyage to plant the first colony in the northern Parts of Virginia; Do by these Presents, solemnly and mutually in the Presence of God and one another, cov-

enant and combine ourselves together into a civil Body Politick, for our better Ordering and Preservation, and Furtherance of the Ends aforesaid. . . .

the Virginia Bill of Rights (1776):

[A]ll men are by nature equally free and independent, and have certain inherent rights, of which, when they enter into a state of society, they cannot by any compact deprive or *divest* their posterity, namely, the enjoyment of life and liberty, with the means of property, and pursuing and obtaining happiness and safety.

the Vermont Declaration of Independence (1777):

We, . . . the inhabitants, [of the New Hampshire grants] are at present without law or government, and may be truly said to be in a state of nature; consequently a right remains to the people of said Grants to form a government best suited to secure their property, well being and happiness.

the Constitution of Massachusetts (written by John Adams in 1779):

The body politic is formed by a voluntary association of individuals. It is a social compact by which the whole people covenants with each citizen and each citizen with the whole people, that all shall be governed by certain laws for the common good. It is the duty of the people, therefore, in framing a Constitution of Government, to provide for an equitable mode of making laws, as well as for an impartial interpretation and a faithful execution of them, that every man may, at all times, find his security in them.

The making of covenants remained a part of the settlement process throughout the days of the land frontier. Men gathered together freely in every one of the thirty-seven states admitted to the Union after the original thirteen to frame constitutions for their governments in the manner of the first compacts establishing local self-government in the New World. Cities and towns were created by compact whenever bodies of men and their families joined together to establish communities devoted to common ends.

With the rise of organizations, the covenant principle was given new purpose. Scientific and reform societies, labor unions, and professional associations as well as business corporations, covenanted with one another to form larger organizations while preserving their own integrities. They initiated a new kind of federalization that continues to this day.

As a consequence of these manifold uses of the covenant idea, the American "instinct" for federalism was extended into most areas of human relationship, shaping American notions of individualism, human rights and obligations, divine expectations, business organization, civic association, and church structure as well as their notions of politics. While there were differences in interpretation of the covenant principle among theologians; between political leaders directly motivated by religious principles and those within a secular political outlook; among New Englanders, residents of the Middle States, and Southerners; and from generation to generation, there was also a broad area of general agreement, which unified all who subscribed to the principle and which set them and their doctrine apart within the larger realm of political theory. All agreed on the importance of popular or republican government, the necessity to diffuse power, and the importance of individual rights and dignity as the foundation of any genuinely good political system. At the same time, all agreed that the existence of inalienable rights was not an excuse for anarchy, just as the existence of ineradicable human passions was not an excuse for tyranny. For them, the covenant provided a means for free men to form political communities without sacrificing their essential freedom and without making energetic government impossible.

The implications of the federal principle are brought home forcefully when it is contrasted with the other conceptions of popular government developed in the modern era. Other revolutionaries in the "Age of Revolutions"—most prominent among them the Jacobins—also sought solutions to some of the same problems of despotism that perturbed the Americans. In their efforts to hurry the achievement of the millennium, however, they rejected what they believed to be the highly pessimistic assumptions of the American constitution makers, that unlimited political power could ever corrupt "the people." They considered only the problem of autocratic despotism. They looked upon federalism and its principle of checks and balances as subversive of "the general will"—their way of expressing a commitment to the organic unity of society which, like their premodern predecessors, they saw as superior to the interests of individuals. They argued that, since their "new society" was to be based on the democratic principle of "the general will," any element subversive of its organic unity would be, ipso facto, antidemocratic.

By retaining notions of the organic society, the Jacobins and their revolutionary heirs were forced to rely upon transient majorities to establish consensus or to concentrate power in the hands of an elite that claimed to do the same thing. The first course invariably led to anarchy and the second to the kind of totalitarian democracy that has become the essence of modern dictatorship. Although "the general

61

will" was undoubtedly a more democratic concept than the "will of the monarch," it has proven to be no less despotic and usually much more subversive of liberty.

The history of the extension of democratic government since the eighteenth century has been a history of the rivalry between these two conceptions of democracy. Because of the challenge of Jacobinism, the meaning of the American idea of federal democracy takes on increased importance.

The American Federal Consensus

The framers of the Constitution of 1787 capitalized on the American instinct for federalism that had already revealed itself in the nationwide organization for the revolutionary struggle and in the first Constitution of the United States. In one sense, they simply tried to improve the American political system within the framework of the covenant idea by creating—as they put it—a "more perfect union."

The results of their work were not accepted uncritically at the time, nor did the results remain unmodified after the ratification of the Constitution. Their emphasis on the "national" as distinct from "federal" aspects of the new Union (the terms are those of *The Federalist*) did not sit well with the majority of the American people, who felt keenly that emphasis on the federal aspects was necessary to keep government limited, taxes low, and liberties secure.

The Anti-Federalists lost their fight to prevent ratification of the Constitution but, by immediately accepting the verdict and entering into the spirit of the new consensus, they soon won over a majority of the American people. After Jefferson's election in 1800, the dominant national theory emphasized the primacy of the states as custodians of the nation's political power, an emphasis that was to be muted from time to time—substantially between 1861 and 1876—but not altered until the twentieth century. This emphasis provided a very hospitable environment for the development of the "states' rights" heresy that colored the actions of Southerners during the Civil War generation.

In reality, the debate over the meaning of the American covenant and its federal principles began anew under the Constitution, has continued ever since, and no doubt will continue as long as the American people remain concerned with constitutional government as an essential element of the American mystique. The debate's very existence adds to the health of the body politic. Yet, from beginning to end, it has remained a debate over interpretation of the federal principle and not over the validity of the principle as such.

Though the debate has involved questions of the first magnitude, it has been carried on within the context of a political consensus that is all the more remarkable for having changed so little in some two hundred years. Rarely, if ever, given verbal expression as a whole, the existence of this consensus is attested to by scores of commentators on the American scene, from Crevecoeur to Max Lerner and from Tocqueville to D. W. Brogan.[17] More impressive testimony is found in the behavior of the American people when that consensus has been threatened. Abandoning their more transient allegiances, they have invariably responded to the call, changing their "normal" patterns of behavior—often to the amazement of observers lacking historical perspective—for others more appropriate to the situation. It is this instinctive understanding of the basics of the American political system that sustains popular government despite the mistakes of transient majorities. The consensus itself is imbued with the spirit of federalism through and through, though it extends much beyond a concern with the strict institutional aspects of the federal system to embrace the ideas of partnership and balance, which, when joined, give birth to the federal principle.

Federalism is not a single way of doing things. As a political way, it provided a basis first for the secession of the southern states, and then for their reintegration into the Union on an equal footing with their northern sisters. Federalism has been interpreted as limiting government action and also as providing the basis for government intervention to force private individuals to behave in a morally correct way. (It is unfashionable for contemporary Americans to endorse John Winthrop's conception of federal liberty, which he defined as the freedom to do what is right.[18] But the recent history of government enforcement of civil rights through U.S. Supreme Court decisions is precisely an example of federal liberty, of the abridgement of the "rights" of individuals to do wrongs to other individuals.)

For three and a half centuries (two under the same Constitution), Americans have managed to follow the federalist way without being conscious they were doing so, except in the narrowest institutional sense. Now, however, the federalist way has come under assault by the twin forces of corporatism and collectivism. These pressures developed in no small measure in response to an individualistic heresy that is no less problematic than the collectivist and corporatist heresies now confronting Americans. An understanding of corporatist models of organization coupled with a set of expectations from government based upon collectivist models—coming at the same time as a reorientation of individualism in the direction of license—have combined to weaken the federalist mainstream of the American experiment. Hence, it becomes vital for those who understand that mainstream to articulate it and to bring it to the attention of those who have taken it for granted and are now puzzled by the transformations taking place in American society.

The year 1976 marked the end of the eleventh generation of American history and of the sixth generation of American independence. It also marked the end of the first generation of the postmodern epoch. The United States, aptly called by Seymour Martin Lipset "the first new nation," was born at the beginning of the modern epoch, achieved its independence as that epoch reached its apex five generations later, and reached maturity during the course of the next five generations until the modern epoch came to an end.[19] The bulk of the adult generation today was raised when it was still possible to talk about the United States as being on the threshold of maturity; as much time separated the founding of the American colonies from the Revolution as separated the Revolution from them, and Americans had not yet experienced a generation of maturity—of great world responsibility, of tragic foreign involvement, or constitutional crisis at home derived from the attempt to substitute imperial for republican styles of behavior in the highest offices of the land. It is different for our children. We have crossed a divide no less formidable than that discussed by Frederick Jackson Turner, when the era of the land frontier came to an end.[20]

The Bible reminds us that every tenth generation begins a new epoch. During the first epoch of American history, the American people forged a unique synthesis of constitutionalism, republicanism, and democracy. As we look back from the vantage point of the newly begun twelfth generation, two generations into the second epoch of American history, we are well advised to consider the character and meaning of the first epoch. Federalism is the glue that has bound constitutionalism, republicanism, and democracy together during the first eleven generations of American history. Like all glue, it has the properties of flexibility and hardness in turn and, once set, tends to be invisible or at least unnoticed in the midst of the materials it has joined together. But without the glue, the materials fall apart. Contemporary Americans have shown that they have no less concern for constitutionalism, republicanism, and democracy than their forefathers did, but it often seems that they are neglecting the bonding agent. If the second epoch of American history is to see the fulfillment of the American promise, then we will have to be as concerned with the bond as we are with the materials themselves.

Notes

1. Martin Diamond, *"The Federalist's* View of Federalism," in George S. Benson, ed., *Essays on Federalism* (Claremont, Calif.: Claremont Men's College, 1961); "Democracy and the Federalist: A Reconsideration of the Framers' Intent," *American Political Science Review* (1959), 64 ff.; "On the Relationship of Federalism and Decentralization," in *Cooperation and Conflict: Readings in American Federalism*, Daniel J. Elazar et al., eds. (Itasca, Ill.: F. E. Peacock, 1969), p. 78 ff.

2. W. W. Crosskey, *Politics and the Constitution* (Chicago: University of Chicago Press, 1953), 2 vols.

3. See Daniel J. Elazar, *Exploring Federalism* (University of Alabama Press, 1987).

4. William Riker, *Federalism: Origin, Operation, Significance* (Boston: Little, Brown, 1964).

5. See, for example, their essays in Daniel J. Elazar, ed., *The Federal Polity* (New Brunswick, N.J.: Transaction Books, 1978). See also, Vincent Ostrom, *A Political Theory of the Compound Republic* (Lincoln: University of Nebraska Press, 1986), rev. ed.

6. Crosskey, *Politics and the Constitution*, for example, vol. 1, chapter 4.

7. Daniel J. Elazar and John Kincaid, eds., *Covenant, Polity and Constitutionalism* (Lanham, Md.: University Press of America and Center for the Study of Federalism, 1980).

8. Donald Lutz, "From Covenant to Constitution in American Political Thought," *Publius* 10, no. 4 (Fall 1980).

9. Charles Hyneman and Donald Lutz, eds., *American Political Writing during the Founding Era, 1760–1805* (Indianapolis, Ind.: Liberty Press, 1983), 2 vols.

10. Gottfried Dietze, *The Federalist: A Classic on Federalism and Free Government* (Baltimore, Md.: John Hopkins University Press, 1960); William B. Allen, "Federal Representation: The Design of the Thirty-Fifth *Federalist Paper*," *Publius* 6, no. 3, (Summer 1976).

11. "The States and Congress Move toward Independence: 1775–1776," *Publius* 6, no. 1 (Winter 1976), pp. 135–44.

12. William James, *A Pluralistic Universe* (Cambridge, Mass.: Harvard University Press, 1977), p. 145.; See also Henry Levinson, "William James and the Federal Republican Principle," *Publius* 9, no. 4 (Fall 1979).

13. Edward Bellamy, *Looking Backward, or 2000–1887* (1888).

14. Herbert Croly, *The Promise of American Life* (New York: E. P. Dutton and Co., Inc., 1963).

15. Alexander Hamilton, John Jay, and James Madison, *The Federalist Papers*, Clinton Rossiter, ed. (New York: Mentor Books, 1961).

16. *Oxford English Dictionary.*

17. See, for example, John Crevecoeur, *Letters from an American Farmer* (1769); Max Lerner, *America as a Civilization: Life and Thought in the United States Today* (New York: Simon and Schuster, 1957).; Alexis de Tocqueville, *De-*

mocracy in America, (New York: Alfred Knopf, 1945).

18. John Winthrop, "A Model of Christian Charity."

19. Seymour Martin Lipset, *The First New Nation* (New York: Basic Books, 1979).

20. Frederick Jackson Turner, "The Significance of the Frontier in American History," paper delivered at conference held in conjunction with the World's Columbian Exposition, Chicago, 1893. Reprinted in *The Frontier in American History* (New York: Holt, 1920).

4
Federalism and the Force of History

David M. Kennedy

Tocqueville's View of American Federalism

Alexis de Tocqueville thought America was a peculiar place. The brilliant young Frenchman visited the United States in the 1830s, the heyday of Jacksonian democracy. He saw Andrew Jackson inspiring a political upheaval that can be understood, at least in part, as a revolt against the incipient (and, by later standards, exceedingly modest) shift of power from the states to the federal government. Jackson exterminated the most notorious federal institution of his day, the Bank of the United States, and he made war on the so-called American System of his political rival, Henry Clay, who wanted the federal government to undertake extensive canal and road-building projects. Jacksonianism represented a familiar impulse in American politics—the urge to keep power distributed among the several states and out of the hands of politicians in Washington. President Ronald Reagan's "new federalism" is an idea that has been around a long time.

Tocqueville generally admired American federalism, and he wrote glowingly of it in his classic treatise, *Democracy in America*. "Nothing is more striking to a European traveller in the United States," he noted, "than the absence of what we term the Government or the Administration"—or what we would today call the federal government or centralized administration.[1] That absence struck Tocqueville with particular force because it contrasted so vividly with the results of the democratic revolution in his native France. There, he recorded, the revolution had had a "double character. . . . Its tendency was at once to republicanize and to centralize."[2] In the name of democracy, French revolutionaries had simultaneously attacked the ancient monarchy and the institutions of provincial government, which Tocqueville described as "incoherent, ill arranged, frequently absurd" organs that "in the hands of the aristocracy. . .had sometimes been converted into the instruments of oppression."[3] America, he concluded, was happily spared that dual character to its own revolution, largely because it enjoyed vigorous, healthy local institutions.

Tocqueville's warm defense of America's unique system of divided sovereignty (*imperium in imperio*, or government within government) has comforted the friends of federalism for a century and a half. They have taken what solace they could from the elegance of his ideas, while enduring a period in which the rude events of history have seemed to conspire against the federalist cause. It has now become high doctrine in some quarters that we have lived through a long epoch in which the central government has steadily and illegitimately aggrandized its power at the expense of state and local prerogatives. This view inspired President Reagan to renew President Jackson's war against centralized administration. Reagan's "new federalism" constitutes a set of policies that apparently seek to reverse the tide of history and to restore a golden age of more agreeable balance between federal and state powers.

Historical Basis of Expanding Federal Power

That doctrine and those policies rest on some questionable historical premises. Unlike Topsy, the federal government did not "just grow," without apparent reason or direction. Federal power has not expanded, as the British Empire was alleged to have done, in a prolonged fit of absent-mindedness, nor has it increased by some perverse process of nationalist usurpation. It is even arguable that federal power has grown exceptionally modestly in this country and that a modern Tocqueville would be just as impressed as his predecessor with the relatively small size of America's central governmental apparatus. Moreover, as I hope to suggest in the following pages, the supposedly golden age to which neofederalists now look back so longingly was not, on close inspection, all that glittery.

Federal vs. State Powers

At about the time Tocqueville was making the preparations for his trip to America, the U.S. Senate witnessed one of the most dramatic debates in its history precisely on the question of the relation between federal and state powers. The famed forensic duel in 1830 between Robert Y. Hayne of South Carolina and Daniel Webster of Massachusetts paraded most of the basic arguments invoked by statesrighters and nationalists in the early decades of our national existence. Hayne maintained that the Constitution was a compact among the states. They thus retained the right to withhold their consent from measures that compromised their sovereign authority. Webster replied that the people as a whole, not the states, had created the Constitution and that the federal government thus had the power to act directly on the people. "It is," he declared, "the people's Constitution, the people's government, made for the people, made by the people, and answerable to the people."[4] Webster here stood on controversial historical ground. The Constitution, it was true, had been ratified in state conventions. Yet the preamble to the document drafted in 1787 read "We the people of the United States"—a significant change from the original draft version of "We the people of the states of"—followed by a list of their names.

Webster further insisted that the republic's early experiment with a radically federalist system, under the Articles of Confederation from 1781 to 1789, had been a political and economic disaster. Without a central mechanism to regulate taxation and commerce, without an executive to enforce legislation, and without a national judiciary to maintain uniform legal standards, chaos reigned. The federal union established by the Constitution of 1789, Webster concluded, had its origins in "the necessities of disordered finance, prostrate commerce, and ruined credit. Under its benign influence, these great interests immediately awoke us from the dead and sprang forth with newness of life."[5]

There was no declared victor in the Webster-Hayne debate, but students of the subject generally agree with Webster that the national experience under the Articles of Confederation defined a degree of decentralization to which all but the most ardent federalists have not cared to return. Memory of that experience thus represents one extreme in the range of opinions about the proper relationship between state and federal sovereignty. It can be argued, however, that as a people we have never succeeded in identifying the other end of that range. We commenced our collective national life with a decided movement away from undiluted localism. That movement has continued to be one of the principal dynamics of our national history. Yet, to use the language of mathematics, we have tried unsuccessfully for nearly 200 years to scale that vector—to determine precisely how far and how fast we wished to take ourselves away from the ramshackle, disarticulated hyperfederalism of the Articles of Confederation.

The Founders' Intentions

The delegates to the Constitutional Convention of 1787 clearly intended to create a preeminent national government. As Jack N. Rakove has observed, that preeminence "seems to have been taken almost for granted," as demonstrated by the lack of controversy over the supremacy clause (Article VI, Paragraph 2).[6] When Edmund Randolph of Virginia proposed that the national legislature should be empowered to act in all cases "in which the harmony of the United States may be interrupted by the exercise of individual [that is, state] legislation," the convention approved without significant dissent.[7] At least one delegate, Butler of South Carolina, was willing to abolish state legislatures altogether. Alexander Hamilton later wrote contemptuously of the prospect of a nation composed "of little jealous, clashing, tumultuous commonwealths, the wretched nurseries of unceasing discord."[8]

If the Founders were clear in their intentions to erect a more centralized government than had obtained under the articles, however, they hesitated in the end to go too far. As Harry N. Scheiber has noted, ideas like those of Randolph and Butler and Hamilton "bespoke a great chasm between the consensus of the nine delegations. . .and the ideas that were popularly shared in the nation at large. For it was widely believed that the states were the only legitimate repositories of supreme power."[9] Thus one of the principal tasks facing the authors of *The Federalist Papers* was to convince the American people that the newly centralized government conceived at Philadelphia did not violently rupture inherited traditions of local rights. James Madison applied himself to that task in several of *The Federalist* essays, but probably nowhere more ingeniously—and ambiguously—than in *Federalist* 39.

There Madison posited that the character of a government should be measured against five criteria: its foundations, the sources, operation, and extent of its ordinary powers, and the procedures by which it might be altered. In a complex, even tortured, argument, Madison concluded that

> The proposed Constitution, therefore,. . .is, in strictness, neither a national nor a federal Constitution, but a composition of both. In its foundation it is federal, not national; in the sources from which the ordinary powers of the government are drawn, it is partly federal and partly national; in the operation of these powers, it is national, not federal; in the extent of them, again, it is federal, not national; and, finally, in the authoritative mode of introducing amendments, it is neither wholly federal nor wholly national.[10]

With much justice does Rakove conclude that "whether the framers of the Constitution anticipated a progressive widening in the effective scope of federal action thus remains one of the most elusive of the many questions asked about their intentions."[11] For at least the next half-century of American history, the framers' intentions were to be vigorously debated. But regardless of the original purposes of those who crafted the federal system, powerful historical forces worked to push American government toward increasing centralization.

The ink on the Constitution of 1787 was scarcely dry when the struggle began anew to redefine the federal-state relationship. As secretary of the Treasury in Washington's cabinet, Hamilton proposed that the federal government should assume responsibility for paying off the Revolutionary War debts of the states. Two considerations lay behind Hamilton's scheme. He believed, first, that the debts had been contracted in a national cause, with disproportionate amounts falling to the various states not because of fiscal logic but because of the vagaries of war. Equity thus was a sufficient reason dictating federal assumption of the states' debts.

Yet Hamilton had a further motive for pushing his plan. He wished to detach the loyalties of wealthy bond holders from the individual states and attach them firmly to the federal government. Assumption amounted to nothing less than a device to ensure that the republic's richest citizens would regard the federal government as the best protector of their economic interests and hence would pledge to Washington, not to the states, their highest political allegiance.

Was this wanton Machiavellianism, the crafty maneuver of a diabolical centralizer with no other aim than enlarging the arena of his own political influence? I think not. Hamilton himself, in *The Federalist*, had anticipated that kind of accusation when he predicted that "an enlightened zeal for the energy and efficiency of government will be stigmatized as the offspring of a temper fond of despotic power and hostile to the principles of liberty." It was too often forgotten, he added, "that a dangerous ambition more often lurks behind the specious mask of zeal for the rights of the people than under the forbidding appearance of zeal for the firmness and efficiency of government."[12] What Hamilton most deeply feared were the consequences of a system, such as that under the articles, in which the central government was neither energetic nor efficient nor firm:

A man must be far gone in Utopian speculations who can seriously doubt that if these States should either be wholly disunited, or only united in partial confederacies, the subdivisions into which they might be thrown would have frequent and violent contests with each other. . . .To look for a continuation of harmony between a number of independent, unconnected sovereignties situated in the same neighborhood would be to disregard the uniform course of human events, and to set at defiance the accumulated experience of ages.[13]

The danger of weak central government, in short, was the danger of civil war—a point on which Hamilton proved painfully prophetic. Indeed, one consequence of the failure to resolve by political means the question of federal supremacy over the states in Hamilton's day was the necessity to settle the issue by fire and sword three generations later. The Civil War was, among other things, a bloody reminder that the problems attendant on America's peculiar system of divided sovereignty were scarcely trivial.

Impulse toward Centralization

The Civil War assuredly laid to rest once and for all the question of the states' right to secede from the Union and thus advanced the republic measurably down the vector that led away from radical decentralization. In addition to resolving, at last, that lingering constitutional question, the Civil War advanced the process of centralization in other, more prosaic but hardly inconsequential ways. Some of the wartime measures by which the federal government extended its role in American life, such as the income tax and military conscription, were abolished at war's end, only to be revived later. Other measures, whose passage owed largely to the temporary absence from Congress of traditionally antifederal southern representatives, survived and permanently altered the character of American society. One thinks immediately of the National Banking System, a product of the exigencies of war financing. It finally ended the confusion and instability that characterized the wildcat, free-wheeling banking practices of the period following Andrew Jackson's successful assault against the Bank of the United States. It provided the country with a significant measure of uniformity in banking practices, a major prerequisite to the sustained economic growth of the last half of the nineteenth century, when much of the nation's industrial foundation was laid. It endured as a major step in the evolution of a true central banking mechanism in the United States, which finally came about with the creation of the Federal Reserve System in 1914. Who today would seriously suggest that any other evolutionary path for the nation's banking structure was superior, or even possible, given the benefits it conferred and the parallel experience of every other economically developed country?

Similarly, the Pacific Railway Acts of 1862 and 1864 made possible the building of the first transcontinental railroad. This legislation stood clearly in the tradition of Henry Clay's proposals to put federal resources behind the construction of what is today called "economic infrastructure." Who today would care to argue that this was an illegitimate federal initiative or that its results were anything other than massively beneficial?

These residues of the Civil War remind us of the important catalyzing effect of all wars, in all societies, in accelerating the process of centralization. This was a lesson of history well known to the Founding Fathers, and it helped to account for their opposition to war and to a large standing military establishment. "If war takes place," Thomas Jefferson wrote, "republicanism has everything to fear. . . .⟨It⟩ is the moment when the energy of a single hand (that is, of a tyrant) shows itself in its most seducing form."[14] Without necessarily subscribing to Jefferson's view that American wars have closed the hand of tyranny over the life of the republic, one must acknowledge that it has been wars, along with comparable crises like the Great Depression, that have provided the most opportune occasions for concentrating additional power in the central government. What should we conclude from this?

First, to the extent that the United States has managed to preserve a less centralized governmental system than other modern nations, the explanation is, perhaps, that we as a people have been singularly spared the scourges of modern warfare that have been visited upon almost every other society. It has not been our collective national virtue or political wisdom, but our fortunate, and entirely accidental, geographical location that has allowed us to maintain for so long our distinctive political system of *imperium in imperio*. Second, the compelling necessities of centralized administration in war illustrate the degree to which decentralization is a luxury. It is a luxury affordable only in circumstances of guaranteed national security, abundant economic resources, and assured social peace. When all—or any—of those conditions are absent, a pressure arises, almost with the regularity of a law of nature, for unitary leadership from the center. This, as Tocqueville knew, was what had happened in the French revolutionary era, when foreign invasion, economic disruption, and the prospect of protracted civil war in France itself required the concentration of political power even in the midst of a democratic revolution.

Insofar as the impulse toward centralization has arisen from crises like war, it is not an impulse that proceeds from some consciously held, ideological agenda that determined men and women have sought to fulfill. It has proceeded, rather, in large measure from the need to respond to events that have vastly overspilled the capacity of local bodies to contain them—events that by their very nature testify to the incapacity of man to will his own destiny fully. Although this observation may not make our long national march away from localism any more palatable, it suggests that history has, perhaps, left us with few alternatives.

Economic Regulation

Nor was it some wanton federal itch to intervene that produced the first of the great peacetime strides toward national regulation of the economy, the Interstate Commerce Act of 1887. The framers of the Constitution could not foresee the growth of the sprawling, complex, continental economy that emerged in America in the century after their deliberations at Philadelphia. For that reason, and because in any case they strove to minimize their departure from the localistic principles of the articles, they did not contemplate the imposition of a national economic policy by the federal government. Chief Justice John Marshall, in *Gibbons* v. *Ogden* (1824), did assert the supremacy of the federal government's right to regulate interstate commerce. His decision had its origins in the effort by New York State to grant to a private company a monopoly of waterborne commerce between New York and New Jersey. Marshall ruled that the state was unconstitutionally asserting authority over interstate commerce that belonged exclusively to the federal government. Although Marshall thus established the principle that the federal power over commerce was supreme (and in the process freed entrepreneurial energies to work on a national scale), in practice that power was not exercised for more than half a century after his decision.

By the 1870s steel rails had replaced waterways as the main arteries of interstate commerce. Corporations that laid tracks across such daunting physical obstacles as the Rockies and the Sierra Nevada were not about to trifle with the artificial political boundaries of state lines. They conducted their affairs in national terms and necessarily called forth a national—that is, federal—regulatory response. Several states did make attempts of their own at railroad regulation. In the 1870s they passed a host of so-called Granger laws, which tried to set maximum freight rates and eradicate the worst abuses of the railroad companies, such as long-short haul rate discrimination, base-point pricing systems, and rebates to favored shippers. Even under the best circumstances, however, these state efforts were bound to be troublesome, as the railroads were forced to contend with a crazy-quilt pattern of different regulations in each of the several states through which their lines ran.

These scattered state efforts came to a screeching halt in 1886, when the Supreme Court, in *Wabash, St. Louis, and Pacific Railway Company* v. *Illinois*, reaffirmed Marshall's ruling in *Gibbons* v. *Ogden* that the individual states had no power to regulate interstate commerce. The state of Illinois, said the court, unconstitutionally intruded upon the federal government's power over commerce when it attempted to prohibit long-short haul rate differentials over a line that ran well beyond the boundaries of Illinois. Unlike the situation in the 1820s, however, it was no longer sufficient to terminate state control over commerce and replace it with nothing. The question was no longer one of releasing entrepreneurial energies but of taming the considerable energies previously released, in the form of huge, powerful railroad corporations. Already bills had appeared in Congress (most notably, and perhaps ironically, the Reagan Bill of 1878) providing for national guarantees of fair competitive practices by the railroads. These efforts had heretofore foundered on the rock of states' rights. But that rock was now submerged by the *Wabash* decision.

Accordingly, in 1887 Congress created the first of the historical federal regulatory agencies, the Interstate Commerce Commission. The record reveals that many railroad companies favored the legislation, because it would make possible a legal environment far more uniform than the patchwork pattern that discrete and disparate state legislatures were weaving. In 1892 Attorney General Richard Olney counseled a railroad company executive that the commission "is, or can be made, of great use to the railroads. . . . ⟨T⟩he older such a commission gets to be, the more inclined it will be found to take the business and railroad view of things,"[15] which, among other things, meant a nationally integrated view of the markets in which the railroads did their business. There was, therefore, nothing inherently antibusiness in transferring regulatory authority over commerce from the states to the federal government—quite the contrary.

A considerable body of scholarly literature is devoted to the thesis that Olney's prediction has proved accurate in some less salubrious ways. It is by now a truism to observe that many regulatory bodies, including the ICC, have developed distressingly close relationships with the very industries they are intended to regulate in the public interest. I do not mean to blink this problem away, but I do want to state emphatically that it does not in any meaningful measure derive from the *federal* character of the regulatory agencies. Dividing regulatory authority among the several states is no remedy to the problem of "capture" of regulatory bodies by the interests they are supposedly overseeing.

The Interstate Commerce Act proved the first wavelet of what turned out to be a small tide of federal regulatory legislation passed during the so-called Progressive Era, which generally spanned the presidencies of Theodore Roosevelt, William Howard Taft, and Woodrow Wilson. These men, together with their progressive contemporaries, undertook to effect a fundamental transformation of American political arrangements. They aimed, as one of their chief spokesmen put it, "to use the government as an agency of human welfare."[16] That meant, above all, investing the federal government with powers commensurate with those that had accumulated in the hands of the great private corporations that had grown up in the preceding half-century. Historians generally date the origins of the Progressive Era from Theodore Roosevelt's swearing in as president in 1901; appropriately enough, it was in the same year that United States Steel became the first American business enterprise to be incorporated with a capital stock valued at over $1 billion. The creation of such an industrial behemoth dramatized the vast growth and accelerating concentration of control in the turn-of-the-century economy—developments that cried out for a proportionate political response.

Political Response to Industrial Abuse

The Republican Roosevelt recognized clearly that his program amounted to nothing less than a radical revision of American political traditions. He regarded his proposed changes as perhaps regrettable but assuredly necessary.

He declared in 1912:

There once was a time in history when the limitation of governmental power meant increasing liberty for the people. In the present day the limitation of governmental power, of governmental action, means the enslavement of the people by the great corporations who can only be held in check through the extension of governmental power. . . .The people of the United States have but one instrument which they can efficiently use against the colossal combinations of business—and that instrument is the Government of the United States.[17]

It is important to stress that Roosevelt was no knee-jerk foe of state prerogatives. He willingly acknowledged that the state governments "where they can be utilized" were effective instruments of the public interest. He often went out of his way to praise the activist government of Wisconsin for making that state "a laboratory for wise social and industrial experiment in the betterment of conditions."[18] But Roosevelt also knew that the twentieth-century American economy—

indeed, the society in all its organic complexity—had evolved to a point where the range of the states' powers was severely limited.

No episode more vividly illustrates the essential soundness of Roosevelt's views than the passage of the Meat Inspection Act in 1906. Every school child has undoubtedly heard the tale of how the publication of Upton Sinclair's *The Jungle*, a stomach-wrenching account of life in the meatpacking houses, prompted a nauseated public to demand governmental oversight of the meatpacking industry. That account is dramatic, but fundamentally inaccurate. The fact is that most packinghouses were subject to state inspections well before 1906. No state, however, dared to enforce too stringent a degree of control for fear of driving the industry beyond its borders. This system of uneven and lax inspection did indeed permit the delivery of some loathsome and even lethal products to the market.

The packers themselves tolerated this situation until, as it happened, about 1906. At that time, several European countries, which made up a major share of the market for American canned meats, began to move toward prohibiting the importation of the too-frequently contaminated American products. Uniform inspection, preferably conducted by a high-level and at least partially disinterested body, was the only way to retrieve that European business.

Thus the system of state inspection failed to protect American consumers and equally failed to protect the manufacturers' position in world markets. Most of the larger packers, when this logic became clear, came to support rather vigorously Roosevelt's proposed legislation to create a federal meat inspection service. The final act, replacing state inspectors with federal ones, constituted a functional response to the structural realities of the industry and benefited consumers and exporters alike. It is difficult to see who, if anyone, was disadvantaged by this new arrangement.

Roosevelt tried to apply similar remedies to a host of similar problems. He suggested several times that Congress create a National Industrial Commission, or Bureau of Corporations, modeled on the Interstate Commerce Commission. In all this, his logic was clear and consistent. He believed, as Walter Lippmann put it in 1914, that the nation must substitute mastery for drift, that laissez faire was an obsolete philosophy, and that federalism was an antiquated apparatus for governing the complex, increasingly interdependent society that America had become.[19] Roosevelt repeatedly, and rationally, called for forging instrumentalities of public power co-extensive with the enormous, continentally scaled agencies of private power that the nation's economic development had spawned.

Effects of War on Federalist Principles

Roosevelt's record as president shows more rhetoric than results in his regulatory efforts, but when the United States entered World War I in 1917, the principles of federalism were once again put to severe test. Despite the political education Roosevelt had labored to impart to his countrymen, the Wilson administration at first tried to organize the economy for war on the old federalist principles. The Council of National Defense, the official mobilization agency created in 1916, started out by organizing defense councils in every state, which in turn were to foster county councils, which again in turn would bring about "community councils" of defense in local school districts. The architects of this nicely symmetric system apparently harbored a quaint faith that the Great War could be fought on a basis similar to that of previous wars: by simply coordinating a large number of separate but essentially equivalent enterprises.

Within a matter of weeks after the American declaration of war, this approach was revealed to be spectacularly irrelevant to the task of organizing the economy of an advanced industrial nation such as America had become by 1917. Effective administrative networks now needed to operate, not along the ancient lines of geography, but along the newly plotted lines of modern economic organization, lines that were functional in character, continental in extent, and pyramidal in their pattern. The old Revolutionary and Civil War practice of requisitioning men and materials from the several states was out of the question. Instead, a host of necessarily federal agencies rapidly emerged, whose very titles designated their appositeness to highly integrated and nationally dimensioned economic sectors: the Food Administration, the Fuel Administration, the Railroad Administration, and the War Industries Board. The Council of National Defense, in fact, degenerated just as rapidly into its constituent state councils. They distinguished themselves throughout the period of American belligerency as local propaganda organs and occasionally as the vehicles of vigilantism and sundry other kinds of assaults on dissenters.

Contrary to popular legend, World War I did not constitute a notably permanent advance toward federal intervention in the economy. Not a single one of the major wartime mobilization agencies survived; most, in fact, were disbanded within days after the armistice of November 11, 1918. The Civil War had left a much more long-lived legacy of centralized governmental agencies than did World War I. For those who cared to reflect on the history of American involvement in the Great War, however, one lesson was clear: when the time came to get serious about accomplishing a national task, the luxury of localism was once again quickly discarded.

The Lessons of the Depression

That lesson was to be pressed much more deeply into the nation's consciousness a little more than a decade later, when the appalling catastrophe of the Great Depression settled down heavily on the land. Again, contrary to popular legend, Franklin Roosevelt's New Deal did not aggressively move to snatch relief and welfare programs away from the states in 1933. By that date, after four years of grinding depression, the states were broke, many of them even on the brink of defaulting on their debt obligations. Those obligations were unusually heavy, as states had typically shunned tax increases and relied instead on bond issues to finance necessary highway construction in the suddenly motorized decade of the 1920s. The credit markets, such as they were, did not smile on the prospect of additional state borrowing. State tax bases, usually comprising levies on real property and sales, offered scant possibilities for expansion. Virtually no states had unemployment compensation plans, and only seventeen had old-age pension plans, most of those dismally underfunded. The states, in short, came begging for federal assistance; they did not have it roughly shoved down their throats.

The New Deal's first relief program, the Federal Emergency Relief Administration, revealed much about the role of the states in welfare programs. The FERA offered matching grants to the states for relief on a three-to-one basis. This meant, first of all, that the distribution of federal money went disproportionately to those states that could readily provide matching funds—and those were not necessarily the states that contained the neediest citizens. James Patterson, in his penetrating study *The New Deal and the States*, concludes that New Deal programs did not alter, but instead strongly reinforced, the existing pattern of the distribution of wealth among the various states.[20] Further, state legislatures that were typically still dominated by rural interests, out of all proportion to demographic and social reality, all too often sought to fund their portion of the matching grants program by cutting their educational and other social-service budgets.

This disillusioning record of the states' inability or unwillingness to assume welfare burdens in an equitable manner helped persuade Congress, when it wrote the Social Security Act of 1935, to make the old-age and survivors' insurance provisions of the legislation almost exclusively federal in character. There were then, as there remain today, compelling reasons for national uniformity of welfare programs, necessarily entailing federal administration. Without it, more generous states justifiably fear becoming saddled with an unfair share of welfare costs, as they become magnets drawing the nation's needy. Poorer states are painfully tempted to deprive their citizens of social services, including adequate education, in order to attract industry by keeping their tax bases low. These fears and temptations thrive in an environment that lacks strong central government direction. The absence of that direction may not lead again, as it did in 1861, to a shooting civil war, but it encourages a kind of federalist economic fratricide that is analogously harmful to the national interest.

One hears much about the increased capacity of the states today to shoulder more responsibilities than they did in an earlier phase of our history. Many states, so the argument runs, have in the past two decades corrected their historic legislative imbalances and modernized their political institutions. Yet it is worth remembering that these undeniably important changes have sprung not from spontaneous local initiatives but from U.S. Supreme Court decisions in the early 1960s, notably *Baker* v. *Carr* (1962), decisions delivered only after the states had abundantly demonstrated their inability to put their own houses in order.

I am reminded here of Tocqueville's sanguine appraisal in the 1830s that American local governments, unlike those in *ancien régime* France, were not incoherent, ill arranged, absurd, or oppressive. It is on some such premise that all cases for federalism, at bottom, must rest. But that premise, on close inspection, turns out to be a beautiful idea murdered by a gang of brutal facts. If we look not to the abstractions of theory but to the actualities of history, we must conclude that the record of government at the state level in our country has not been an exceptionally coherent, well-arranged, or rational affair. Too often, as in the case of regulating interstate economic enterprises, the states have proved incapable of coping with problems whose real dimensions far exceed their geographic boundaries or political powers. Too often, as in the case of Depression welfare programs, they have been unwilling or unable to cope with problems even well within their strictly political jurisdiction. Too often, as in the case of gross rural overrepresentation in their legislatures, the states have perpetuated patent political absurdities.

The Myth of Local Government

Indeed, far too often, the record sadly reveals, the states have been the instruments of oppression. When asked to respect our "traditions" of local government, one is tempted to recollect Winston Churchill's alleged description of the "traditions" of the British Navy as embracing grog, sodomy, and the lash. Tocqueville did much to establish a largely mythical image of the benevolence of American local governments. Yet in the very year that Tocqueville landed in America,

Nat Turner ignited his bloody mutiny against the slave system in Virginia. At almost the same moment, several hundred miles to the north, William Lloyd Garrison launched the most notorious of the abolitionist newspapers, *The Liberator*. Only by ignoring these developments could Tocqueville persist in the fiction that American local governments were immune to the blight of oppression. His ignorance, in retrospect, seems almost willful. "Amongst the novel objects that attracted my attention during my stay in the United States," he proclaimed in the very first sentence of his famous tract, "nothing struck me more forcibly than the general equality of condition among the people"—this at a time when the population contained 2 million black slaves.[21]

Three decades after Tocqueville's day it was the federal government that finally excised the cancer of slavery from the American body politic, a radical surgery performed over the armed and militant objections of eleven states. Disarmed in defeat, those states (and others) proved no less militant in the postwar decades in denying full equality to many of their citizens. The Fourteenth Amendment, passed in the 1860s to prevent the de facto resurgence of slavery, lay dormant and ineffective for nearly a century, but in our own time its equal protection clause has proven a powerful weapon against racism and discrimination. That weapon, by its very nature, has been wielded by the federal government, which has been the great, if sometimes sputtering engine of our national ideal of equality.

The Antidote for Divisive Faction

Sound structural reasons, with foundations deeply underlying our history, help to account for that federal role. During the debate over ratifying the federal Constitution of 1787, James Madison, in *Federalist* 10, made one of the most famous contributions to American—indeed to Western—political theory. Among the foremost advantages of the proposed federal union, Madison urged, was "its tendency to break and control the violence of faction. . . . By a faction I understand a number of citizens, whether amounting to a majority or a minority of the whole, who are united and actuated by some common impulse of passion, or of interest, adverse to the rights of other citizens, or to the permanent and aggregate interests of the community."[22] The causes of "faction" Madison took to be seated irremovably in human nature; one might deal, therefore, only with the task of controlling its effects. Madison cited two means by which the new union might check the innate human tendency toward faction. First, the new government was to be "republican" rather than democratic—that is, it was to place governing powers in the hands of a small number of persons rather than investing them directly in the hands of all. Second, and far more important in Madison's view,

> is the greater number of citizens and extent of territory which may be brought within the compass of republican than of democratic government. . . .⟨I⟩t is this circumstance principally which renders factious combinations less to be dreaded. . . .Extend the sphere and you take in a greater variety of parties and interests; you make it less probable that a majority of the whole will have a common motive to invade the rights of other citizens. . . .Hence, it clearly appears that the same advantage which a republic has over a democracy in controlling the effects of faction. . .is enjoyed by the Union over the States composing it.[23]

In more modern idiom, one might summarize Madison's message by saying that it is only the central government, by virtue of its aloofness from local passions, that has proven capable, even if only occasionally, of lifting us above petty parochialisms and sometimes vicious prejudices and holding us up to our own highest ideals—especially the ideal of equality. The extent of our federal government may not be the result of the founders' purposeful design, nor even the product of some logic long latent in the Constitution. But neither is it historical accident nor an altogether unwelcome historical legacy. Central government is a highly evolved mechanism. Like all products of evolutionary processes, it has grown in a series of functional responses to real social and economic needs. Uniquely the political organ of all American citizens, the federal government has been the agent of much that is praiseworthy, and it has often been the instrument of our national conscience as well. To dismantle it in the name of a probably antiquated and assuredly discriminatory "localism" is more than modern America should be made to endure.

Notes

1. Alexis de Tocqueville, *Democracy in America* (New York: Mentor Books, 1956), p. 62.

2. Ibid., p. 72.

3. Ibid., pp. 71–72.

4. William Jennings Bryan, ed., *The World's Famous Orations*, vol. 9 (New York: Funk and Wagnalls, 1906), p. 46.

5. Ibid., pp. 61–62.

6. Jack N. Rakove, "The Legacy of the Articles of Confederation," *Publius: The Journal of Federalism*, vol. 12 (Fall 1982), p. 62.

7. Max Farrand, ed., *The Records of the Federal Convention of 1787*, vol. 1 (New Haven: Yale University Press, 1911), p. 21.

8. Clinton Rossiter, ed., *The Federalist Papers* (New York: New American Library, 1961), p. 73.

9. Harry N. Scheiber, "Federalism and the Constitution: The Original Understanding," in Harry N. Scheiber and Lawrence Friedman, eds., *American Law and the Constitutional Order* (Cambridge: Harvard University Press, 1978), p. 86.

10. Rossiter, *Federalist Papers*, p. 246.

11. Rakove, "Legacy of the Articles of Confederation," p. 63.

12. Rossiter, *Federalist Papers*, p. 35.

13. Ibid., p. 54.

14. Thomas Jefferson to Thaddeus Kosciusko, February 21, 1799, in Edward Dumbauld, ed., *The Political Writings of Thomas Jefferson* (Indianapolis: The Liberal Arts Press, 1955), p. 182.

15. Quoted in Grant McConnell, *Private Power and American Democracy* (New York: Alfred A. Knopf, 1966), p. 284.

16. William Allen White quoted in David M. Kennedy, ed., *Progressivism: The Critical Issues* (Boston: Little, Brown, 1971), p. vii.

17. Theodore Roosevelt, *Progressive Principles: Selections from Addresses Made during the Presidential Campaign of 1912*, ed. Elmer H. Youngman (New York: Progressive National Service, 1913), pp. 216–17.

18. Ibid., p. 142.

19. See Walter Lippmann, *Drift and Mastery: An Attempt to Diagnose the Current Unrest* (New York: M. Kennerly, 1914).

20. James T. Patterson, *The New Deal and the States: Federalism in Transition* (Princeton, N.J.: Princeton University Press, 1969).

21. Tocqueville, *Democracy in America*, p. 26.

22. Rossiter, *Federalist Papers*, p. 78.

23. Ibid., p. 83.

5

Madison and Modern Federalism

Jean Yarbrough

The question, How federal is the Constitution? is both legal and political. It is legal because the Constitution prescribes certain federal features. In a more important sense, however, it is political, since the Constitution does not delineate precisely the extent of the powers to be exercised by the state and national governments, but leaves that practical determination to politicians acting in accord with popular wishes. When we reflect upon this question, we must consider not only the text itself, but also the meaning of those broad silences in the intentions of the men who framed it and who implemented its provisions during the early formative years of the republic. In creating our unique federal system, the framers were compelled to consider the more crucial question, How federal *should* the Constitution be?

Examining the views of the framers provides us with insight into the nature of the American republic. As we shall see, the men of 1787 held views surprisingly current today about how federal the republic should be. The chief architects of the Constitution were radical nationalists who had little patience or sympathy with the arguments in favor of states' rights. Their experience under the Articles of Confederation had persuaded them that the safety and liberty of the people depended not upon the state governments, or even upon a balance between the states and the central government, but upon a preponderance of power in the national government. From this perspective, the framers' understanding of federalism seems surprisingly relevant: they anticipated the steady expansion of the national government into state affairs and approved of it, holding it essential to the preservation of liberty and the common good.

In a consideration of the framers' intentions, the views of James Madison are especially significant, since he is widely regarded as the

I thank my colleague, Professor Raymond Tatalovich, for his helpful comments and suggestions.

Father of the Constitution and is a principal author of *The Federalist*. Yet concentrating on Madison's political thought raises a problem. Within a few years after the Constitution was ratified, Madison began to retreat from the ultranationalist position he espoused in 1787 and broke with this position completely in 1798. The enactment of the Alien and Sedition Laws changed Madison from a vigorous nationalist to a genuine supporter of the newly invented modern federal principle embodied in the Constitution. In the Virginia Resolutions of 1798, Madison defended the states as bulwarks of liberty in an extended republic. Although Madison was later to regret some of the more ambiguous and incendiary language of the resolutions, he never repudiated the document (at least as he clarified it in 1800), and in fact, at the height of the Nullification Crisis during the 1830s, he insisted that the Virginia Resolutions were consistent with his understanding of the Constitution. (For good reason he remained silent on the question of the compatibility of the resolutions with his views at the Federal Convention.)

In this defense of the modern federal over the national principle, there is an even more recent parallel. Just as Madison repudiated the nationalist policies of the Federalist administrations as inconsistent with republican liberty, so too, and for similar reasons, did the Reagan administration seek to dismantle the nationalizing policies of the New Deal and the postwar period. Consequently, Madison's political thought takes on special significance. In considering Madison's intentions as a framer, we cannot limit ourselves to his views in 1787, which he later explicitly rejected as an authoritative explication of the Constitution. We must also consider his emerging views of federalism as he sought "to adapt an untried instrument of government to a new country"[1] and, in the light of his experience, as he reflected upon the institutions necessary to preserve republican government.

Madison the Nationalist: *The Federalist*

Students of the American republic are frequently surprised to learn that the leading framers of the Constitution vehemently opposed the compromises that led to the creation of the modern federal principle. The failure of the states to protect against the evils of majority faction under the Articles of Confederation led supporters of free government to try to replace the confederal form with an energetic national government in which the powers of the states would be greatly diminished. To this end, Madison proposed that the states be stripped of their political representation in the national government and that the national legislature be equipped with an absolute veto over all state acts.[2]

Had Madison's original proposals succeeded, the Constitution would have established a basically consolidated national government in which the states were no more than administrative agencies, stripped of all vestiges of sovereignty. As "corporations dependent upon the General Legislature," the states would continue to perform "beneficial" tasks and to be "subordinately useful," but they would have no power to challenge the national government. This is the relationship that municipal governments now bear to the states, and Madison recommends it as the model for relations between the states and the national government.[3]

Clearly, then, Madison cannot be credited with having invented the modern federal principle. Rather, modern federalism seems to have resulted from compromises that made it unsatisfactory to nationalists and federalists alike. As Martin Diamond has persuasively shown,[4] however, political thinkers in the eighteenth century understood federalism very differently from the way we do. We see federalism as a unique principle whereby political power is constitutionally divided between the states and the national government, each sovereign in its own sphere. In contrast, the earlier thinkers considered federalism synonymous with confederacy, consequently requiring political arrangements more closely resembling a league of nations than a government. For this reason, nationalists like Madison saw the federalism of the Constitution as an unsteady compound of irreconcilable confederal and national elements. They fought to secure the ratification of the Constitution in spite of its federal elements and in the hope that the nationalist principle would ultimately prevail.

In *The Federalist* papers, Madison joined forces with another radical nationalist, Alexander Hamilton, to explain the text of the Constitution in a way that would allay the fears of its critics. To this end, the authors employed a number of rhetorical devices that exaggerate the powers reserved to the states and minimize those entrusted to the national government. Thus, it is not surprising that Madison later sought to qualify the authority of *The Federalist* to explain the principles of the federal Constitution. As he put it, *The Federalist* "did not foresee all the misconstructions which have occurred; nor prevent some that it did foresee."[5] Although he does not mention any specific misconstructions, a careful reading of *The Federalist* suggests that its view of federalism is a prime candidate.

The Federalist exaggerates the significance of the states in several ways. In No. 45, for example, Madison insists that the powers reserved to the states are so "numerous and indefinite" that the states, rather than the national government, pose a threat to liberty. More-over, since these powers touch on "all those objects which, in the ordinary course of affairs, concerned the lives, liberties, and prop-erties of the people," the citizens were likely to remain more attached to their state governments, thus ensuring their primacy within the federal system. Finally, in No. 44, Madison argues that the states may play an important role in restraining encroachments by the national government. Defending the constitutional grant of implied powers, Madison argues that should the Congress exceed its trust and "ex-ercise powers not warranted by its true meaning," the state legisla-tures "will ever be ready to mark the innovation, to sound the alarm to the people, and to exert their local influence in effecting a change of federal representatives."[6]

This, then, is the surface argument of The Federalist regarding the scope of state powers. It is an argument Madison and Hamilton could make, partly because of their genuine fear that the states did indeed retain too many powers. Madison and Hamilton did not doubt the power of combined states, or even of a single great state, to act. What they feared was that the states would be ruled by majority factions and would therefore endanger the rights of the minority and the common good.[7] But it is also an argument they could make, in spite of their preference for a more consolidated government, because they expected these dangerous centrifugal tendencies to diminish in the future. The Federalist makes this argument circumspectly, for obvious reasons.

To the careful reader, however, The Federalist suggests that as the people become more familiar with the workings of the national gov-ernment and experience the benefits of its superior administration, they will see that their rights are better secured by the national gov-ernment and will welcome its extension to "what are called matters of internal concern."[8] In this way, the people will gradually overcome their natural tendency to love best what is near and transfer their loyalty and affection to the national government. The subtle message of The Federalist is that the states will gradually decline, not because the national government will usurp their powers, but ironically be-cause "in republics strength is always on the side of the people."[9] And in the future, the people are more likely to look to the national government to provide for their safety and happiness.

The Federalist hints at its true opinion of federalism in a different way as well. In other papers, where one expects to find a discussion of federalism, there is sometimes silence, or at best a grudging rec-ognition. Speaking in No. 62 of the equal participation of the states in the Senate—a key feature of the old federalism that Madison opposed at the Federal Convention—Madison dismisses it as "the lesser evil," "evidently the result of compromise," "not call[ing] for much discussion."[10] In keeping with assertions made elsewhere in *The Federalist*, Madison here describes his support for the federal elements of the Constitution as a "sacrifice," which he prudently makes expecting that in the future popular support for the federal elements of the Constitution will wane. (To a considerable extent, of course, *The Federalist*'s expectations have been borne out. The Seventeenth Amendment provides for the direct election of senators by the people of each state. More recently, constitutional amendments have been proposed to abolish the partly federal Electoral College in favor of a national popular election. Whether the widespread popular indifference to federalism has resulted in the beneficial results *The Federalist* anticipated, however, remains to be seen.) Similarly, *The Federalist* quickly passed over Article IV, which guarantees the constitutional existence of the states as political associations, and Article V, which protects the equality of state suffrage in the Senate, placing it beyond even the mostly federal amending process.

Even the radically nationalistic Madison nevertheless recognized that there were limits to how far these consolidating tendencies could go. If in the future the people did become more attached to the national government, Madison understood, the states would still be necessary—not because they are vital to liberty, but because there are limits to how far national power can be effectively administered in a large republic.[11] In other words, Madison believed the utility of the states served primarily the purpose of good administration rather than the purpose of federalism. This is but a more cautious restatement of Madison's own observation at the Federal Convention that if it were possible for the national government "to extend its care to all the minute objects which fall under the cognizance of the local jurisdictions,"[12] there would be no need to retain the states at all. In this view, the role of the states is purely administrative.

At first glance this distinction between federalism and administrative decentralization may not seem significant, but in fact the differences between these two modes of decentralization are rooted in opposing views of how republican liberty and the common good are best secured. Modern federalism rests on the assumption that a large consolidated government is itself a danger to liberty, since it dangerously strengthens the executive branch and threatens to transform the republic into monarchy—if not in name, at least in principle. Federalism further assumes that, despite the internal checks provided by the separation of powers and the representative principle, the national government may also infringe upon the rights of the people and the powers of the states. Accordingly, advocates of federalism support the *constitutional* division of power between the states and the national government, so that each may stand guard against the undue accumulation and abuse of power by the other.

Administrative decentralization, by contrast, rests on the assumption that the states as political associations are the primary threat to republican liberty because they are too small to encompass the diversity of interests and opinions necessary to preserve freedom. Consequently, advocates of administrative decentralization oppose the division of sovereignty upon which federalism rests as a needless invitation to discord and faction.[13] They prefer instead to reduce the states to local corporations, whose sole purpose is to carry out the legislative projects mandated by the national government. According to this view, liberty is best secured by a preponderance of power in the national government, provided its powers are properly distributed and its representatives accountable to the people. The states play no major part in preserving republican liberty.

Although these latter views are only hinted at in *The Federalist*, they are consistent with Madison's proposals a few months earlier at the Federal Convention. We find a problem, however, if we rely on the views of leading framers such as Madison at the Federal Convention or in *The Federalist* to explain the federal principle: their nationalist recommendations were not incorporated into the plan of government that emerged from the Philadelphia convention and that *The Federalist* is supposedly elucidating. The Constitution does not reduce the states to mere creatures of the national government but preserves them as political bodies with a considerable portion of sovereignty. As Harry Jaffa observes, the effect of these federal provisions upon the nature of the union is significant:

> The Constitution as originally ratified and subsequently amended seems to have pledged, even against the constituent powers of the people, as embodied in the amending article, to maintain the states in their prescribed constitutional role, as indestructible components of the Union. However flexibly this role might be interpreted, there would appear to be a design in the Constitution destined forever to prevent the people of the United States from becoming a mere numerical aggregate.[14]

Granting that the allocation of these powers is largely a political question, there is still a difference between what *The Federalist* prefers and what the Constitution authorizes.

Moreover, if *The Federalist* exaggerates the powers reserved to the states (while subtly indicating its own preferences), it tends to minimize the powers entrusted to the national government, making them appear more consistent with the constitutional division of sovereignty required by the federal principle. Nowhere is this more evident than in its treatment of implied powers. Critics feared that a broad construction of the "general welfare" and "necessary and proper" clauses would become the "pernicious engines by which their local governments were to be destroyed and their liberties exterminated."[15]

Against the abuse of implied powers in particular, and the totality of powers vested in the national government in general, *The Federalist* offers three arguments. First, the national government will have no incentive to encroach upon the powers reserved to the states because the objects of state legislation are so slight: "the regulation of the mere domestic police of a state appears to me to hold out slender allurements to ambition."[16] This, however, is a curious assurance. Second, the proper distribution of powers and representative accountability will ensure that the national government stays within its bounds. In this regard, Madison suggests that the states may play a role in preserving liberty, but he also implies that resort to the state governments to arouse the citizens to elect new and more faithful representatives is a last resort and will probably be unnecessary.[17] Finally, proper rules of constitutional interpretation will restrain the national government. Implied powers extend only to those objects that the Constitution entrusts to the national government, and the Constitution does not give the national government power over all objects. Nevertheless, within its rightful sphere, Madison takes an almost Marshallian view of implied powers. As he wrote in No. 44,

> No axiom is more clearly established in law, or in reason, than that wherever the end is required, the means are authorized; wherever a general power to do a thing is given every particular power necessary for doing it, is included.[18]

Upon reflection, such a construction of implied powers seems more consistent with Madison's nationalism than it does with the federal principle.

Through these rhetorical devices, *The Federalist* helped to secure the ratification of the Constitution. But it did so at the cost of obscuring the nature of the union. By simultaneously exaggerating the federal and minimizing the national elements of the new Constitution, *The Federalist* managed to suggest one answer to the question, How federal is the Constitution? and an altogether different response to the question, How federal *should* (and, in the future, will) the Constitution be? Because these two views are at odds with each other, however, we must determine which view is the wiser one. On this question, the later political thought of James Madison is instructive.

Madison's Move toward Federalism

Although it is customary to view the framing and ratification of the Constitution as the culmination of the revolutionary era, these activities would have been of no avail if the men of the revolution had not been able to make the new constitution work. Moreover, on the all-important issue of how the Constitution would be used to shape the new republic, the chief authors of The Federalist parted company almost immediately over the funding of the national debt and the national assumption of state war debts. Although this issue is not directly related to the federal-national controversy, it is important because it suggests that what Madison initially objected to was not simply an energetic national government but the oligarchic tendencies of Hamilton's nationalism.[19] Madison objected to Hamilton's schemes because he feared they would undermine republican government by creating a powerful economic interest based on speculation rather than on industry. In other words, Madison's initial concern was with preserving republican government through the encouragement of a certain kind of citizen.

Like his fellow Virginian Thomas Jefferson, Madison believed that the agrarian way of life was most suitable for maintaining republican institutions, but unlike Jefferson he never dogmatically opposed commercial and manufacturing interests.[20] Indeed, he supported the imposition of a tariff to raise revenue and promote infant industry during the First Congress and continued to back such measures throughout his career. He was opposed not to commerce, but to speculation, for he thought the latter rewarded the nonindustrious and encouraged the formation of habits and character inimical to the preservation of the republic.[21]

In the dispute over the National Bank, Madison's fears of oligarchy and consolidation came together. Again, as in the funding issue, Madison feared the creation of a speculative moneyed interest tied to the national government.[22] Perhaps for this reason Madison began to fear the strengthening of the national government through a broad construction of implied powers. Whereas Madison had seen no danger from consolidation in 1787, as early as 1791, he began to worry that the centralization of powers would strengthen the executive branch and transform the republic into monarchy. Madison no doubt feared this process would be aided by the antirepublican forces created by Hamilton's economic policies. In another essay written

91

during this period for the *National Gazette*, the Republican party newspaper, Madison described American society as currently divided into two parties, the republican and the antirepublican. The antirepublicans are "those who, from particular interest, from natural temper, or from habits of life, are more partial to the opulent than to other classes of society." Such men are dangerous because they are persuaded "that mankind are incapable of ruling themselves" and can be ruled only by rank, money, or force. Consequently, they seek to direct the government "by degrees" into fewer hands until it approximates "an heredity form."[23]

To repeat, Madison's opposition to the policies of the Federalist party can be explained chiefly as a rejection of the oligarchic thrust of Hamilton's economic program. It was not a wholesale repudiation of an energetic national government. For the extent that the administration's vigorous policies did not threaten the preservation of republican mores and institutions, Madison continued to support them. As we have seen, he favored the tariff and argued that the encouragement of manufacturing was a legitimate exercise of Congress's power to regulate trade. Similarly, Madison's support for the Bill of Rights during the First Congress was not meant to weaken the national government. On the contrary, Madison sought to extend the Bill of Rights to prohibit *state* abridgement of the rights of press, conscience, and trial by jury.[24] Moreover, in the debates, Madison made it clear that the purpose of the Ninth and Tenth Amendments was not "to change the principles of government." For this reason, he opposed the addition of the word "expressly" to the Tenth Amendment, which would have reserved to the states "the powers not *expressly* delegated to the United States by the Constitution." As Madison argued, "It was impossible to confine a government to the exercise of express powers; there must necessarily be admitted powers by implication."[25] In other words, Madison did not object to the principles of implied powers, although his position, beginning in the 1790s, recognized the tension between a broad construction of such powers and republicanism, especially federal republicanism.

Madison attempted to resolve this dilemma by arguing that the Constitution be amended rather than broadly interpreted whenever additional powers were necessary. And although this solution proved too cumbersome and was not adopted, Madison's predictions about the effect of broad construction have proved true.

Momentous as these issues were in shaping "what form of government and what type of society were to be produced in this country,"[26] by far the greatest controversy—and the one that proved decisive in changing Madison's political thought—was not over Hamilton's economic policies,[27] but over John Adams's politics. Although Hamilton's programs obviously prepared the way, the turning point for Madison was the Alien and Sedition Acts of 1798. Opposing these laws in the Virginia Resolutions written in the same year, Madison for the first time fully acknowledged the advantages of modern federalism in sustaining republican government.

The main point of the Virginia Resolutions is that the Constitution creates a national government of specific and enumerated powers. These powers result "from the compact to which the states are parties." Whenever the national government oversteps its bounds by construing its powers too broadly, the states must restrain it. In such cases the states, as parties to the compact,

> have the right and are in duty bound to interpose for arresting the progress of the evil and for maintaining in their respective limits the authorities, rights and liberties appertaining to them.[28]

That Madison here decisively breaks with his ultranationalist principles of 1787 does not, however, mean that he became an advocate of states' rights. The change in Madison's political thought is seemingly less radical, but actually more so. The states' rights position is a restatement of the old confederal-national dichotomy that insists that sovereignty cannot be divided. According to this view, the states as political bodies are sovereign, and the Constitution is a compact uniting sovereign states. Consequently, in all disputes arising under the Constitution, each state, as a sovereign party to the Constitution, has the right to judge the issue for itself.[29] Modern federalism, by contrast, holds that it is not the states as political units that are sovereign, but the people in the states. Acting in their sovereign capacity, they establish a constitution that divides sovereign power between the states and the national government to secure their safety and happiness. In this view, the Constitution is supreme over both governments and the people over the Constitution. It is the recognition that sovereignty can be divided among different governments that makes possible the emergence of modern federalism as a distinct political principle, rather than a compound of warring confederal and national principles.

Yet as Madison himself belatedly recognized, his argument in the Virginia Resolutions was ambiguous and could be (indeed, it later was) read, however mistakenly, as a defense of states' rights. The resolutions do maintain that the powers of the national government result from a compact among the states and that, "in case of a deliberate, palpable, and dangerous exercise of other powers not granted by the compact," the states have the right and duty to "interpose." These inflammatory phrases led every state from Maryland north to reject the constitutional theory enunciated in the Virginia (and even more radical Kentucky) Resolutions.[30] Consequently, Madison found it necessary to issue "A Report on the Virginia Resolutions" in 1799– 1800, clarifying his position.

In the report, Madison acknowledges that the expression "states" is vague and ambiguous, but he insists that in the resolutions the term refers to "the people composing those political societies in their highest sovereign capacity." This is the sense in which the Constitution was submitted to the "states," in which the Constitution was ratified by the "states," and in which the "states" are the parties to the compact under which the national powers arise.[31] Accordingly, when the national government exceeds its rightful powers, only the parties to the compact, that is, the people in the states in their highest sovereign capacity, can determine that the Constitution has been breached. It is true that the judicial branch is the "last resort" as far as the three branches of government go, but it is not the last resort "in relation to the rights of the parties to the constitutional compact" because it too is a delegated trust.[32] Moreover, the judiciary may also overleap its rightful bounds, and in such cases the parties to the Constitution must judge. Still, Madison explains, there is nothing unconstitutional in these "great and extraordinary cases" when the people assert their ultimate right. For their views as embodied in the declarations of their respective state legislatures are merely "expressions of opinion."[33] They are not intended to supplant the judgment of the courts, but to arouse the citizens to "promote a remedy according to the rules of the Constitution."

Madison does not prescribe what the remedy should be, leaving the particular choice to the states. His discussion, however, makes clear that he means repealing the Alien and Sedition Acts, either by electing new representatives or by amending the Constitution according to the procedure set forth in Article V. In this way, the Virginia Resolutions are not only consistent with the Constitution, but are actually "expedient." As Madison points out, most state constitutions recommend "a frequent recurrence to fundamental principles . . . [to] safeguard against the danger of degeneracy." The Virginia Resolutions preserve the Constitution by returning to these first principles in speech. As a "declaratory recurrence to the principles of the Revolution,"[34] the resolutions alert the people of the United States to dangerous encroachments upon their rights in time to avoid an actual return to first principles.

The Virginia Resolutions mark a turning point in Madison's political thought because they signify his recognition (made only rhetorically in *The Federalist*) that the states can play a role in maintaining liberty in a large republic. As constitutionally protected political societies, they possess the power to resist the tendency toward consolidation. Moreover, although ultimately it is the people in the states who are sovereign, the states contribute to the happiness of the people by preserving the constitutional balance necessary to protect republican liberty.

As we have already seen, there is another aspect to modern federalism. Insofar as modern federalism derives from the constitutional division of sovereignty between two levels of government, it means not only a political role for the states, but also a more restrictive interpretation of implied powers for the national government. Here too Madison modified his views to make them compatible with his emerging appreciation of federal theory. In contrast to the position he held as late as 1791 in the debate on the constitutionality of the bank, Madison came to view the mere existence of the states as a limitation on national powers (despite his opposition to the bank, he observed that "interference with the power of the States was no constitutional criterion of the power of Congress"[35]). This is apparent in a letter to Judge Roane in 1819, following the *McCulloch* decision, in which Madison reversed his earlier position and argued that "the very existence of these local sovereignties is a controul on the pleas for a constructive amplification of the powers of the General Government." Nevertheless, Madison made it clear that his intention was not to hamstring the national government. What he sought was a prudent middle ground:

There is certainly a reasonable medium between expounding the Constitution with the strictness of a penal law, or other ordinary statute, and expounding it with a laxity which may vary its essential character, and encroach on the local sovereignties with which it was meant to be reconcilable.[36]

These principles of modern federalism were to guide Madison's political actions and writings for the rest of his life. As president, he followed, in most of his policies, the lines he laid down while in opposition to the Federalists. He sought to reconcile the need for an energetic national government with his commitment to preserve the powers and authorities of the states. As in 1789, he supported a moderate tariff to aid the development of manufacturing after the War of 1812. He also continued to hold that internal improvements were not authorized by the Constitution. Accordingly, he again proposed that the Constitution be amended to provide Congress with a clear grant of power for such projects.[37] Madison's federalism, then, did not prevent him from seeking to enlarge the powers of the national government in those areas he considered its proper domain. But it did keep him from relying upon a broad construction of the Constitution to justify such policies. In only one area during his presidency did Madison reverse himself, and that was on the issue of the Second National Bank. As Professor Marvin Meyers points out, however, Madison's endorsement of the bank in 1816 was not based on a new reading of the Constitution, but on precedent, public opinion, and congressional policy.[38]

Madison's political career is commonly seen as divided into three periods: an early nationalist stage, a middle states' rights period, and a final reaffirmation of nationalist principles. It is true that Madison did not systematically spell out the principles of modern federalism, or distinguish them carefully enough from states' rights, on the one hand, and nationalism, on the other. As we have already argued, though, the break in Madison's political thought, embodied in the Virginia Resolutions, does not rest upon states' rights, but upon modern federalism. We shall now argue that Madison's late political thought, that is, 1830 onward, can be understood not as a return to his nationalism of the 1780s, but as consistent with the federalist principles he enunciated in 1798.

Madison and Modern Federalism

In the 1830s when opponents of the tariff invoked the Virginia (and Kentucky) Resolutions in defense of nullification, Madison responded by publishing his letter to Edward Everett in the *North American Review*, denouncing any connection between the resolutions of 1798 and the South Carolina doctrine. Madison explained that the Constitution spells out the procedures by which unconstitutional usurpations of power may be overturned: first, an appeal to the judiciary and then a change of government by electing more faithful representatives. If these ordinary provisions fail, the proper course is to amend the Constitution. If this too is unsuccessful, a state may resort to force, but this is an extraconstitutional step. There is no constitutional sanction for defiance of the law by a single state. Indeed, such a doctrine reverses the express provisions of the amending article, which require three quarters of the states to change the law. According to the proponents of nullification, one state may invalidate a federal law unless overruled by three quarters of the states. The doctrine of nullification is not sound constitutional interpretation because it fails to distinguish between: (1) the state governments and the states in their capacity as parties to the Constitution; (2) the rights of the parties individually and collectively; and (3) constitutional and unconstitutional modes and objects of interposition.[39]

In his final reflections on the nature of the union, written in 1835–1836, Madison even more emphatically defended the Virginia Resolutions against the claims of states' righters. It is there that he drew the theoretical distinction between states' rights and modern federalism most clearly:

> The main pillar of nullification is the assumption that sovereignty is a unit, at once indivisible and unalienable; that the states therefore individually retain it entire as they originally held it, and consequently that no portion of it can belong to the United States.[40]

If it is correct to say that the early Madison was also inclined to doubt that sovereignty could be divided and, consequently, to champion a consolidated national government, his discovery that it *could* be divided became the guiding principle of his political life after 1798.

Indeed, far from returning to these early nationalist views, Madison implicitly rejected them by repudiating the authority of the Federal Convention to explicate the meaning of the Constitution. Madison gives us an early hint of this thinking in the Report on the Virginia Resolutions. Here he does not openly reject the authority of the Federal Convention but instead invokes the intentions of those who *ratified* the Constitution.[41] Later, Madison made the point explicit:

> As a guide in expounding and applying the provisions of the Constitution, the debates and incidental decisions of the Convention can have no authoritative character. . . . [T]he legitimate meaning of the Instrument must be derived from the text itself; or if a key is to be sought elsewhere, it must not be in the opinions or intentions of the Body which planned and proposed the Constitution, but in the sense attached to it by the people in their respective State Conventions where it received all the authority it possesses.[42]

In Madison's view, the opinions of the framers at the Federal Convention should not be authoritative because they were wrong and, more particularly, he was wrong about the dangers facing republican government. As he explained in a letter to J. G. Jackson, written in 1821:

> That most of us carried into the Convention a profound impression produced by the experienced inadequacy of the

old Confederation, and by the monitory examples of all similar ones ancient & modern, as to the necessity of binding
the States together by a strong Constitution is certain. . . .
This view of the crisis made it natural for many in the Convention to lean more than was perhaps in strictness warranted by a proper distinction between causes temporary as
some of them doubtless were, and causes permanently inherent in popular frames of Govt. . . . For myself, having
from the first moment of maturing a political opinion, down
to the present one, never ceased to be a votary of the principle
of self-Govt: I was among those most anxious to rescue it
from the danger which seemed to threaten it; and with that
view was willing to give a Govt resting on that foundation,
as much energy as would ensure the requisite stability and
efficacy. It is possible that in some instances this consideration may have been allowed—a weight greater than subsequent reflection within the Convention, or the actual
operation of the Govt. would sanction.[43]

In other words, the change in Madison's political thought is largely
a response to the changing political situation. In 1787, Madison saw
the chief danger to liberty arising from a central government too weak
to control the factious designs of the states. Accordingly, at the Federal
Convention, he advocated a national government with far greater
powers than the Constitution created.

By 1798, however, the situation had changed. So successful had
the Federalist administration been in asserting the powers of the national government that Madison recognized that the principle of federalism embodied in the Constitution against his wishes could in fact
play an important role in preserving republican institutions. It was
this revised view of the dangers to republican liberty that led Madison
to reject the authority of the nationalist Federal Convention in favor
of the more federal ratifying conventions—conventions that, he also
believed, represented the authentic sense of the people of the United
States about the nature of the union.

In summary, there is only one significant change in Madison's
political thought, and that is from his consolidationist nationalism to
modern federalism. After 1788, Madison's political thought may be
understood as a fairly consistent attempt to resolve political issues
within the framework of modern federalism. Such a position allowed
him to support a vigorous national government, but it also required
him to reconcile this position with the rights and authority of the
states. Modern federalism gave him the flexibility to move between

national and state demands, depending upon his assessment of a particular issue. But because he did not systematically choose the national government over the states, or the states over the national government, or elucidate sufficiently the principle that allowed him to defend the legitimate spheres of both, he is sometimes accused of inconsistency or even opportunism. Most of these criticisms lose their force, however, when we consider Madison's political thought from the perspective of modern federalism.

Madison on Slavery

In one area, however, Madison's political judgment in asserting the rights of the states over the national government is indefensible: the issue of slavery. Then as now, the issue of race relations proves to be the least susceptible to federal solutions, perhaps because, as Tocqueville recognized, it is the most difficult political problem.

The specific issue on which Madison's federal principle falters is the Missouri Compromise. Asked by Robert Walsh, the Philadelphia journalist, for his views on the constitutionality of the issues involved in the compromise, Madison replied that the Constitution did not give Congress the power to control the migration of slavery within the United States or to make opposition to slavery a condition for the admission of a new state to the union. He even went so far as to question whether Congress had the power to prohibit slavery in the territories. Although Madison acknowledged that Congress did have the power "to make provisions *really* needful or necessary" in the territories,[44] he questioned whether slavery belonged in this category:

It may be inferred that Congress did not regard the interdict of slavery among the needful regulations contemplated by the constitution; since in none of the Territorial Governments created by them, is such an interdict found.[45]

As Marvin Meyers points out, however, this tortured interpretation ignored "the sweeping grant of federal power in the territorial clause and the long-standing precedent of the Northwest Ordinance as re-enacted by the First Congress."[46] In defense of his reading of the Constitution, Madison recurs to the proceedings of the state ratifying conventions, though the one speech he cites by James Wilson in the Pennsylvania debates suggests that Wilson did believe Congress had such a power.[47] Thus, Madison's interpretation does violence not only to the Constitution, but also to the intentions of the men who ratified it.

In his letter to Walsh, Madison argued for the constitutionality of his position, as well as for its "expediency." He speculated that the spread of slavery, by reducing the number of slaves in any one territory, might hasten their emancipation. Madison rejected the possibility that such a policy might eventually lead to a majority of slave-holding states with the power to rescind the limitations imposed on slavery in the Constitution. In this instance it is impossible to escape Meyers's conclusion that "the problem of slavery demanded a kind of political genius and daring and conviction beyond the capacity even of Madison."[48] Meyers brilliantly describes the irony of Madison's position and shows how it ultimately led to the crisis that culminated in the Civil War:

> Madison and Jefferson—the most distinguished spokesmen for the Revolutionary tradition in the South—concluded that the real issue in the Missouri debates was not the spread of slavery across the Mississippi but rather the creation of a sectional party by disguised Federalists who appealed to Northern anti-slavery sentiments in order to divide and conquer the Republicans. The ultimate price of injecting slavery into national politics, they warned, would be the disruption of the Union.

> The Compromise of 1820 admitted Missouri without anti-slavery conditions and, contrary to Madison's advice, banned slavery in the Louisiana Territory north of 36° 30'. The *reversal* of that policy of exclusion by Congress and the Supreme Court in the 1850's finally precipitated the division that Madison had feared: the formation of a new Republican party in the North out of the anti-slavery elements of the major national parties.[49]

If Madison's federalism resulted in perverse consequences for the greatest moral and political crisis facing the union, we are justified in asking whether his earlier nationalist views were not in fact wiser, even if they do not accurately describe the government created by the Constitution or reflect the sense of the nation as expressed in the Ratifying Debates.

Reflection upon this matter raises two questions. The first is clearly a matter of speculation: would not the reduction of the states to something like administrative agencies of the national government have averted the Civil War? At first glance, this suggestion seems plausible, for the particular way in which the crisis developed was inextricably bound up with federalism and the question of sovereignty. But the issue of slavery—especially in the early nineteenth century, after Southerners had ceased to view "the peculiar institution" as a necessary evil in irreconcilable tension with the principles of the Declaration of Independence and had begun to defend it as a positive good—cut so deeply into the moral and political fiber of the republic that it seems unlikely that the South would have acquiesced in any scheme to limit slavery, even if the national government had the clear-cut power to do so. In that case, the Civil War would have been a strictly sectional, rather than sectional and federal, affair.[50]

The second question raised is, Would not administrative decentralization preserve the rights of the people better than our system of divided sovereignty? Here again, it seems at first as if the rights of the minority might be better protected if the national government were equipped with an absolute veto over all state laws. The national government may also infringe upon the rights of the people, however, and this danger increases where there are no limits upon the expansion of national power. The Federalist's confident prediction that the national government would be restrained from undue encroachment upon the rights of the people has been belied by the growth of the national bureaucracy, the willingness of the Supreme Court to uphold, and in many cases augment, the scope of national powers, and a firm conviction on the part of public opinion leaders that such developments are both beneficial and irresistible. Even with their status constitutionally protected, the states have not been able to resist the steady expansion of national powers into areas historically reserved to them. This is because, as we suggested at the outset, the distribution of powers between the states and the national government is not set in stone but can be flexibly interpreted to meet the political demands of the time. Why power has shifted to the national government and what this shift means for President Reagan's New Federalism and for the preservation of republican institutions in general, we shall now consider.

Reagan's New Federalism

In his late political thought, Madison cast the states as bulwarks of liberty, jealousy guarding against encroachments by the national government. In our own day, the states have become more like the administrative agencies Madison envisioned in his early nationalist period. Moreover, far from resisting this development, as Madison hoped they would, the states have for the most part welcomed it.[51] The reason for this change is simple and has more to do with economics than political theory.

According to James Q. Wilson, massive federal involvement in state affairs was made possible with the passage of the Sixteenth Amendment in 1913. The Sixteenth Amendment "allowed the federal government to levy an income tax on citizens and thereby to acquire access to vast sources of revenue." The consequences were immediate and enormous: "Between 1914 and 1917, federal aid to states and localities increased a thousandfold. By 1948, it amounted to over one tenth of all state and local spending; by 1970, to over one sixth."[52]

In other words, the relationship of the states to the national government began to shift when the states became the recipients of federal dollars. At first, the states determined the purposes for which these grants would be used; in this way, airports, highways, and other such programs were funded. This period of "cooperative federalism," as it was called, allowed the states the best of both worlds— it increased political power and autonomy, without increasing costs. In the 1960s, however, the federal relationship began to change. Increasingly, the president and his advisers defined the purposes of the grants and targeted money for specific "national" programs on poverty, ecology, and the like. As Wilson points out, all this was done "not necessarily over the objections of the states, but without any initiative from them."[53]

At the same time, state autonomy was more seriously eroded by the expansion of the federal bureaucracy and judiciary into its affairs. As Nathan Glazer explains, the bureaucracy, which is charged with the responsibility for implementing legislation, has increasingly substituted its own more activist view of what the law should accomplish, rather than being guided by the intentions of Congress.[54] Moreover, because the bureaucracy lacks the "power of the purse," the states must bear the burden of these additional requirements and procedures. Similarly, the federal courts have ordered the states to implement costly programs in prison reform, public housing, welfare, and other such areas, leaving the states to raise money.[55] President Nixon's Revenue-Sharing program attempted to return to the states a measure of autonomy by replacing grants-in-aid for specifically defined projects with bloc grants, which would allow them greater leeway in spending federal funds. The program failed to contain encroachments by the federal bureaucracy and judiciary, however.

In contrast with these recent Democratic and Republican efforts, President Reagan's New Federalism is actually an attempt to restore what he believes to be the original meaning of federalism, by returning to the states the responsibility for administering and ultimately *for funding* some of the more controversial programs of the Great Society. For this reason, the states have been reluctant to endorse it. They are understandably reluctant to choose between raising taxes and alienating taxpayers, or eliminating programs and angering organized interests.[56] From the point of view of the states, the issue is not primarily one of liberty or autonomy, but of expense. As long as the people expect the government to maintain—to say nothing of increase—its present level of services, the states will continue to insist upon a more generous federal "partnership," and the provisions of the Constitution are sufficiently flexible to sustain such an interpretation if this is what the people want. Moreover, the New Federalism does not directly redress the principal complaints the states have against the national government. Although the New Federalism may curb bureaucratic encroachments, it cannot immediately restrain judicial activism.[57]

Aside from the issue of cost, which, however important, is not and never can be the animating principle of a free society, are there any advantages to be gained from a renewed respect for the federal principle?

Let us consider briefly the three arguments made on behalf of federalism. First, throughout most of its history, federalism has been important for its role in promoting civic virtue. According to the republican tradition, which stretched from ancient Greece and Rome through the Renaissance republics to the seventeenth-century English commonwealth and up to America in 1776, the primary purpose of federalism was to secure the advantages of a small republic while providing for defense through confederal association. It was thought that republican governments had to remain small in order to secure civic virtue. By civic virtue was meant a willingness to sacrifice private interests for the sake of the common good. This individual dedication to the whole was achieved in part through the active participation of the citizens in public affairs; direct democracy taught them to care for what they held in common. Federalism made direct democracy possible by allowing the republic to remain small; consequently, federalism was essential to the republic because it promoted civic virtue.[58]

This aspect of the republican tradition Madison and the framers of the Constitution consistently and emphatically rejected. Indeed, Madison's defense of the American republic in *Federalist 10* rested upon precisely the opposite assumption: it was not smallness, but largeness that would rescue republican government, and it would do so by substituting representation for direct participation. As Madison explained in *Federalist 63*, "The true distinction between . . . [the ancient republics] and the American governments lies *in the total exclusion of the people in their collective capacity* from any share in . . . their government." He then adds,

This distinction however qualified must be admitted to leave a most advantageous superiority in favor of the United States.

103

But to ensure to this advantage its full effect, we must be careful not to separate it from the other advantage, of an extensive territory. For it cannot be believed that any form of representative government could have succeeded within the narrow limits occupied by the democracies of Greece.[59]

The large republic, based on representation and modern federalism, may be superior to the small republic, but not because it promotes civic virtue in the traditional sense. Although modern federalism does bring the government "closer" to the people (and thus encourages civic virtue in a looser sense), it does not provide the citizens with an active and continuing opportunity to participate in public affairs. Direct democracy is no more possible at the state level than it is at the national level.[60]

The one place where direct democracy is possible in the extended republic is in the localities. Local governments have always been schools for civic virtue. By providing ordinary citizens with the opportunity to share in the activities of the republic within their competence, these political associations mitigate the worst effects of liberal individualism. Moreover, these self-governing communities put teeth into the claim that the people are the source of all political power, for alone among the institutions of the republic they allow men and women to exercise political power and responsibility jointly with their fellow citizens. But the federal system extends only to the constitutional division of sovereignty between the states and the national government; it does not include the localities, which are legally "creatures of the states." Consequently, federalism promotes civic virtue in this sense only indirectly, by further decentralizing political power to the localities. Moreover, since the localities have no constitutional power to resist state encroachments, even the indirect role of federalism in promoting civic virtue is problematic.[61]

Federalism as embodied in the American Constitution cannot, then, be understood primarily within the framework of the classical republican tradition, though it continues to promote such ends in an attenuated way. Rather, modern federalism must be judged by its role in preserving the *liberal* republic, with its commitment to the protection of individual liberty through largeness and diversity. In other words, modern federalism must be judged by how well it promotes pluralism on the one hand and liberty on the other.

Modern federalism strengthens diversity, by providing the different cultures generated in the large republic with the political power to preserve their social, moral, and political differences.[62] It is federalism that makes possible the astounding diversity of state laws on gambling, drinking, marriage, the family, divorce, education, and criminal law, to name some of the more important areas reserved to the states. Thus, federalism permits Nevada's liberal laws on gambling, drinking, and divorce to coexist with the stricter views of neighboring Utah, without offending the dominant culture of either.

Closely related to the role of federalism in preserving our national diversity is the opportunity it affords the states to experiment in public policy, thereby confining the damage if unsuccessful, and serving as a model if successful. This experimentation does not preclude some degree of federal oversight to ensure that the constitutional rights of individuals are not violated, but it does require the national government to respect the heterogeneity and experimentation generated by the federal principle as essential elements of preserving the extended republic.

Finally, and most important, modern federalism is necessary for republican government because it helps prevent the concentration of political power in the national government. For, to a much greater degree than Madison recognized when he warned against the dangers of consolidation, the nationalization of public policy has shifted political power from elected representatives in Congress to an unelected bureaucracy within the executive and to the courts. This is because "it is hard for Congress, owing to its clumsy and complex procedures, to control implementation of legislation by the executive, and it is impossible for Congress to control the interpretation by the judiciary of that implementation."[63] Consequently, we have national policy increasingly made by unelected officials, often against the wishes of the majority. Seen in this light, the rediscovery of the federal principle (though not necessarily in the form of the New Federalism) is long overdue. Federalism, to be sure, does not guarantee the protection of individual rights. Those who oppose federalism because they fear a majority tyranny in the states, however, are advised to consider that a national tyranny is also possible—and more dangerous.

Notes

1. Joseph Charles, *The Origins of the American Party System* (New York: Harper & Row, 1961), p. 3.

2. James Madison to George Washington, April 16, 1787, in Marvin Meyers, ed., *The Mind of the Founder: Sources of the Political Thought of James Madison* (Indianapolis: Bobbs-Merrill Company, Inc., 1973), pp. 94–98. Also, Max Farrand, ed., *The Records of the Federal Convention*, 4 vols. (New Haven: Yale University Press, 1937), vol. 1, pp. 27, 165.

3. Farrand, *Records of the Federal Convention*, vol. 1, pp. 357–58.

4. Martin Diamond, "*The Federalist's* View of Federalism," in George C. S.

Benson, ed., *Essays in Federalism* (Claremont, Calif.: Institute for Studies in Federalism, 1962), pp. 21–64.

5. Madison to Jefferson, Feb. 8, 1825, in Meyers, *Mind of the Founder*, pp. 444–45.

6. James Madison, Alexander Hamilton, and John Jay, *The Federalist*, ed. Jacob B. Cooke (Middletown, Conn.: Wesleyan University Press, 1961), No. 45, p. 313; No. 44, p. 305.

7. *Federalist* No. 10.

8. *Federalist* No. 27, p. 174, and No. 46, p. 317. Also, Diamond, *"Federalist's* View of Federalism."

9. *Federalist* No. 31, p. 198.

10. *Federalist* No. 62, pp. 416–17.

11. *Federalist* No. 46, p. 317; also, Diamond, *"Federalist's* View of Federalism," pp. 56, 61, 64.

12. Farrand, *Records of the Federal Convention*, vol. 1, pp. 357–58.

13. Diamond, *"Federalist's* View of Federalism," p. 60n., but cf. *The Founding of the Democratic Republic* (Itasca, Illinois: F. E. Peacock Publishers, Inc., 1981), p. 131.

14. Harry V. Jaffa, "Partly Federal, Partly National: On the Political Theory of the American Civil War," in *The Conditions of Freedom* (Baltimore: The Johns Hopkins University Press, 1975), pp. 161–62.

15. *Federalist* No. 33, p. 204.

16. *Federalist* No. 17, p. 105.

17. *Federalist* No. 44, p. 305.

18. Ibid., pp. 304–305; cf. Marshall's reasoning in McCulloch v. Maryland, 4 Wheat. 316, 4 L. Ed. 579 (1819).

19. Charles, *American Party System*, p. 6ff. Also, Paul C. Peterson, "The Problem of Consistency in the Statesmanship of James Madison: The Case of the Virginia Report," in Ralph A. Rossum and Gary L. McDowell, eds., *The American Founding: Politics, Statesmanship, and the Constitution* (Port Washington, N.Y.: Kennikat Press, 1981), pp. 122–34.

20. Cf. Madison's essay, "A Republican Distribution of Citizens," in Meyers, *Mind of the Founder*, pp. 241–43, and Jefferson, Query No. XIX, in William Peden, ed., *Notes on the State of Virginia* (Chapel Hill: University of North Carolina Press, 1954), p. 165.

21. See Madison's comment in *The Writings of James Madison*, ed. Gaillard Hunt, 9 vols. (New York: G. P. Putnam's Sons, 1906), vol. 6, p. 86, where he supports "withholding unnecessary opportunities from a few, to increase the inequality of property by an immoderate, and especially unmerited accumulation of riches."

22. Harry V. Jaffa, "The Nature and Origin of the American Party System," in *Liberty and Equality* (New York: Oxford University Press, 1965), p. 27; also, Peterson, "Problem of Consistency," p. 123.

23. Meyers, *Mind of the Founder*, esp. p. 247.

24. Ibid., p. 217. See also, Herbert Storing, "The Constitution and the Bill of Rights," in Robert A. Goldwin and William A. Schambra, eds., *How Does*

the Constitution Secure Rights? (Washington, D.C.: American Enterprise Institute, 1985), pp. 15–35.

25. As cited in Alpheus T. Mason and William M. Beaney, *American Constitutional Law: Introductory Essays and Selected Cases* (Englewood Cliffs, New Jersey: Prentice-Hall, Inc., 1964), p. 105.

26. Charles, *American Party System*, p. 6.

27. Nathan Schachner, *The Founding Fathers* (New York: Capricorn Books, 1961), p. 467. On the Sedition Acts, Schachner quotes Hamilton as saying they contained provisions "which, according to a cursory view, appear to me highly exceptionable. . . . I hope sincerely the thing may not be hurried through. Let us not establish a tyranny. Energy is a very different thing from violence."

28. Henry Steele Commager, ed., *Documents of American History* (New York: Appleton-Century-Crofts, Inc., 1948), vol. 1, p. 182.

29. Jaffa, "Partly Federal, Partly National," esp. p. 173.

30. Commager, *Documents of American History*, vol. 1, p. 184.

31. Meyers, *Mind of the Founder*, pp. 302–3.

32. Ibid., p. 306.

33. Ibid., p. 346.

34. Ibid., p. 307.

35. Cited in Walter Berns, "The Meaning of the Tenth Amendment," in Robert A. Goldwin, ed., *A Nation of States* (Chicago: Rand McNally, 1962), p. 157n.

36. Meyers, *Mind of the Founder*, p. 461; also, p. 328.

37. Ibid., pp. 379, 390.

38. Ibid., pp. 390–91.

39. Ibid., p. 543.

40. Ibid., p. 568.

41. Ibid., p. 327.

42. Madison to Thomas Ritchie, September 15, 1821, in Farrand, *Records of the Federal Convention*, vol. 3, pp. 447–48.

43. Ibid., p. 449.

44. Meyers, *Mind of the Founder*, p. 410 (emphasis added). The Constitution grants the power to "make all needful rules and regulations respecting the territory . . . of the United States." Cf. Madison's opposition to the addition of "expressly" to the Tenth Amendment, and his additional qualification "*really*" in this matter.

45. Ibid.

46. Ibid., p. 405.

47. Farrand, *Records of the Federal Convention*, vol. 3, p. 437. Professor Meyers gives the full text of the letter, but omits the footnote referred to here.

48. Meyers, *Mind of the Founder*, p. 398.

49. Ibid., p. 406.

50. Daniel J. Elazar, "Civil War and the Preservation of American Federalism," *Publius: The Journal of Federalism*, vol. 1, no. 1.

51. Morton Grodzins and Daniel J. Elazar, "Centralization and Decentral-

ization in the American Federal System," in Goldwin, *Nation of States*, p. 18ff.

52. James Q. Wilson, "The Rise of the Bureaucratic State," in Nathan Glazer and Irving Kristol, eds., *The American Commonwealth, 1976* (New York: Basic Books, Inc., 1976), p. 91.

53. Ibid., p. 92. This section draws heavily on Wilson's analysis.

54. Nathan Glazer, "Towards an Imperial Judiciary?" in ibid., p. 113.

55. Ibid., esp. pp. 117–19.

56. Especially since it was the national government that created these "clients" (Wilson, "Rise of the Bureaucratic State," p. 92). Moreover, owing to judicial activism, the states would be obliged to maintain a far greater range of services than they did in the 1950s.

57. Glazer, "Towards an Imperial Judiciary?" pp. 112–23. Here, however, the judicial self-restraint and respect for federalism exhibited in recent opinions of Justices Rehnquist and O'Connor is a hopeful sign.

58. John Agresto, "Virtue and Republicanism, 1776–1787," *The Review of Politics*, vol. 39, no. 4, pp. 473–504.

59. *Federalist* No. 63, p. 428.

60. *Federalist* No. 9, pp. 52–53.

61. *Federalist* No. 44, p. 305.

62. Meyers, *Mind of the Founder*, pp. 431–32. Also, Daniel J. Elazar, *Cities of the Prairie* (New York: Basic Books, Inc., 1970).

63. Glazer, "Towards an Imperial Judiciary?" p. 113.

6

The Idea of the Nation

Samuel H. Beer

I have a difference of opinion with President Reagan. We have all heard of the president's new federalism and his proposals to cut back on the activities of the federal government by reducing or eliminating certain programs and transferring others to the states. He wishes to do this because he finds these activities to be inefficient and wasteful. He also claims that they are improper under the U.S. Constitution— not in the sense that the courts have found them to violate our fundamental law, but in the larger philosophical and historical sense that the present distribution of power between levels of government offends against the true meaning and intent of that document.

In justification of this conclusion, he has relied upon a certain view of the founding of the republic. In his inaugural address he summarized its essentials when he said: "The federal government did not create the states; the states created the federal government." This allegation of historical fact did not pass without comment. Richard Morris of Columbia took issue with the president, called his view of the historical facts "a hoary myth about the origin of the Union," and went on to summarize the evidence showing that "the United States was created by the people in collectivity, not by the individual states." No less bluntly, Henry Steele Commager of Amherst said the president did not understand the Constitution, which in its own words asserts that it was ordained by "We, the People of the United States," not by the states severally.

We may smile at this exchange between the president and the professors. They are talking about something that happened a long time ago. To be sure, the conflict of ideas between them did inform the most serious crisis of our first century—the grim struggle that culminated in the Civil War. In that conflict, President Reagan's view— the compact theory of the Constitution—was championed by Jefferson Davis, the president of the seceding South. The first Republican president of the United States, on the other hand, espoused the national theory of the Constitution. "The Union," said Abraham Lincoln, "is older than any of the states and, in fact, it created them as States. . . . The Union and not the states separately produced their independence and their liberty. . . . The Union gave each of them whatever of independence and liberty it has."

As stated by President Lincoln, the national idea is a theory that ultimate authority lies in the United States. It identifies the whole people of the nation as the source of the legitimate power of both the federal government and the state governments.

The national idea, however, is not only a theory of authority but also a theory of purpose, a perspective on public policy, a guide to the ends for which power should be used. It invites us to ask ourselves what sort of a people we are, and whether we are a people, and what we wish to make of ourselves as a people. In this sense the national idea is as alive and contentious today as it was when Alexander Hamilton set the course of the first administration of George Washington.

Like the other Founders, Hamilton sought to establish a regime of republican liberty, that is, a system of government which would protect the individual's rights of person and property and which would be founded upon the consent of the governed. He was by no means satisfied with the legal framework produced by the Philadelphia convention. Fearing the states, he would have preferred a much stronger central authority, and, distrusting the common people, he would have set a greater distance between them and the exercise of power. He was less concerned, however, with the legal framework than with the use that would be made of it. He saw in the Constitution not only a regime of liberty but also, and especially, the promise of nationhood.

He understood, moreover, that this promise of nationhood would have to be fulfilled if the regime of liberty itself was to endure. The scale of the country almost daunted him. At Philadelphia, as its chief diarist reported, Hamilton "confessed that he was much discouraged by the amazing extent of the Country in expecting the desired blessings from any general sovereignty that could be substituted." This fear echoed the conventional wisdom of the time. The great Montesquieu had warned that popular government was not suitable for a large and diverse country. If attempted, he predicted that its counsels would be distracted by "a thousand private views" and its extent would provide cover for ambitious men seeking despotic power.

One reply to Montesquieu turned this argument on its head by declaring that such pluralism would be a source of stability. In his famous Tenth Federalist, James Madison argued that the more extensive republic, precisely because of its diversity, would protect popular government by making oppressive combinations less likely. Hamilton did not deny Madison's reasoning, but perceived that something more than a balance of groups would be necessary if the more extensive republic was to escape the disorder that would destroy its liberty.

Hamilton summarized his views in the farewell address he drafted for Washington in 1796. Its theme is the importance of union. But this union does not consist merely in a balance of groups or a consensus of values, and certainly not merely in a strong central government or a common framework of constitutional law. It is rather a condition of the people, uniting them by both sympathy and interest, but above all in "an indissoluble community of interest as *one nation*."

Hamilton's nationalism did not consist solely in his belief that the Americans were "one people" rather than thirteen separate peoples. The father of the compact theory himself, Thomas Jefferson, at times shared that opinion, to which he gave expression in the Declaration of Independence. The contrast with Jefferson lay in Hamilton's activism, his belief that this American people must make vigorous use of its central government for the task of nation building. This difference between the two members of Washington's cabinet, the great individualist and the great nationalist, achieved classic expression in their conflict over the proposed Bank of the United States. Jefferson feared that the bank would corrupt his cherished agrarian order and discovered no authority for it in the Constitution. Hamilton, believing that a central bank was necessary to sustain public credit, promote economic development, and—in his graphic phrase—"cement the union," found in a broad construction of the "necessary and proper" clause of Article I ample constitutional authorization. Looking back today and recognizing that the words of the Constitution can be fitted into either line of reasoning, we must sigh with relief that President Washington, and in later years the Supreme Court, preferred the Hamiltonian doctrine.

Hamilton was not only a nationalist and centralizer, he was also an elitist. Along with the bank, his first steps to revive and sustain the public credit were the full funding of the federal debt and the federal assumption of the debts incurred by the states during the war of independence. These measures had their fiscal and economic purposes. Their social impact, moreover, favored the fortunes of those members of the propertied classes who had come to hold the federal and state obligations. This result, while fully understood, was incidental to Hamilton's ultimate purpose, which was political. As with the bank, that purpose was to strengthen the newly empowered cen-

111

tral government by attaching to it the interests of these influential members of society. Hamilton promoted capitalism, but not because he was a lackey of the capitalist class—indeed, he once wrote to a close friend, "I hate moneying men." His elitism was subservient to his nationalism.

In the same cause he was not only an elitist, but also an integrationist. I use that term expressly because of its current overtones, wishing to suggest Hamilton's perception of how diversity need not always be divisive, but may lead to mutual dependence and union. Here again he broke from Jefferson, who valued homogeneity. Hamilton, on the other hand, planned for active federal intervention to diversify the economy by the development of commerce and industry. His great report on manufactures is at once visionary and far-seeing— "the embryo of modern America," a recent writer terms it.

Hamilton is renowned for his statecraft: for his methods of using the powers of government for economic, political, and social ends. But that emphasis obscures his originality, which consisted in his conceptualization of those ends. His methods were derivative, being taken from the theory and practice of state builders of the seventeenth and eighteenth centuries, from Colbert to Pitt. Hamilton used this familiar technology, however, to forward the unprecedented attempt to establish republican government on a continental scale. In his scheme the unities of nationhood would sustain the authority of such a regime. By contrast, those earlier craftsmen of the modern state in Bourbon France or Hohenzollern Prussia or Whig Britain could take for granted the established authority of a monarchic and aristocratic regime. They too had their techniques for enhancing the attachment of the people to the prince. But in America the people were the prince. To enhance their attachment to the ultimate governing power, therefore, meant fortifying the bonds that united them as a people. If the authority of this first nation-state was to suffice for its governance, the purpose of the state would have to become the development of the nation. This was the distinctive Hamiltonian end: to make the nation more of a nation.

The national idea, so engendered, confronted three great crises: the crisis of sectionalism, culminating in the Civil War; the crisis of industrialism, culminating in the Great Depression and the New Deal; and the crisis of racism, which continues to rack our country.

In the course of the struggle with sectionalism, John C. Calhoun defined the issue and threw down the challenge to nationalism when he said: ". . . the very idea of an *American People*, as constituting a single community, is a mere chimera. Such a community never for a single moment existed—neither before nor since the Declaration of

Independence." This was a logical deduction from the compact theory, which according to Calhoun's system made of each state a "separate sovereign community."

His leading opponent, Daniel Webster, has been called the first great champion of the national theory of the union. If we are thinking of speech rather than action, that is true, since Hamilton's contribution, although earlier, was in the realm of deeds rather than words. Webster never won the high executive power that he sought, and the cause of union for which he spent himself suffered continual defeat during his lifetime. But the impact on history of words such as his is not to be underestimated. "When finally, after his death, civil war did eventuate," concludes his biographer, "it was Webster's doctrine, from the lips of Abraham Lincoln, which animated the North and made its victory inevitable." Webster gave us not only doctrine, but also imagery and myth. He was not the narrow legalist and materialistic Whig of some critical portraits. And if his oratory is too florid for our taste today, its effect on his audiences was overpowering. "I was never so excited by public speaking before in my life," exclaimed George Ticknor, an otherwise cool Bostonian, after one address. "Three or four times I thought my temples would burst with the gush of blood." Those who heard him, it has been said, "experienced the same delight which they might have received from a performance of *Hamlet* or Beethoven's Fifth Symphony." Poets have been called, "the unacknowledged legislators of the world"; this legislator was the unacknowledged poet of the young republic.

To say this is to emphasize his style; but what was the substance of his achievement? Historians of political thought usually, and correctly, look first to his memorable debate with Senator Robert Hayne of South Carolina in January of 1830. Echoing Calhoun's deductions from the compact theory, Hayne had stated the doctrine of nullification. This doctrine would deny to the federal judiciary the right to draw the line between federal and state authority, leaving such questions of constitutionality to be decided—subject to various qualifications—by each state itself.

In reply Webster set forth with new boldness the national theory of authority. Asking what was the origin of "this general government," he concluded that the Constitution is not a compact between the states. It was not established by the governments of the several states, or by the people of the several states, but by "the people of the United States in the aggregate." In Lincolnian phrases, he called it "the people's Constitution, the people's government, made for the people, made by the people and answerable to the people," and clinched his argument for the dependence of popular government on nationhood with that memorable and sonorous coda, "Liberty and union, one and inseparable, now and forever."

These later passages of his argument have almost monopolized the attention of historians of political thought. Yet it is in an earlier and longer part that he developed the Hamiltonian thrust, looking not to the origin but to the purpose of government. These initial passages of the debate had not yet focused on the problems of authority and nullification. The question was rather what to do with a great national resource—the public domain, already consisting of hundreds of millions of acres located in the states and territories and owned by the federal government. Large tracts had been used to finance internal improvements, such as roads, canals, and schools, as envisioned by Hamilton and ardently espoused by the previous president, John Quincy Adams.

When Webster defended such uses, citing the longstanding agreement that the public domain was for "the common benefit of all the States," Hayne made a revealing reply. If that was the rule, said he, how could one justify "voting away immense bodies of these lands—for canals in Indiana and Illinois, to the Louisville and Portland Canal, to Kenyon College in Ohio, to Schools for the Deaf and Dumb." "If grants of this character," he continued, "can fairly be considered as made for the common benefit of all the states, it can only be because all the states are interested in the welfare of each— a principle, which, carried to the full extent, destroys all distinction between local and national subjects."

Webster seized the objection and set out to answer it. His task was to show when a resource belonging to the whole country could legitimately be used to support works on "particular roads, particular canals, particular rivers, and particular institutions of education in the West." Calling this question "the real and wide difference in political opinion between the honorable gentleman and myself," he asserted that there was a "common good" distinguishable from "local goods," yet embracing such particular projects.

In these passages the rhetoric is suggestive, but one would like a more specific answer: what *is* the difference between a local and a general good? Suddenly Webster's discourse becomes quite concrete. His approach is to show what the federal government must do by demonstrating what the states cannot do. Using the development of transportation after the peace of 1815 for illustration, Webster shows why a particular project within a state, which also has substantial benefits for other states, will for that very reason probably not be undertaken by the state within which it is located.

"Take the instance of the Delaware breakwater," he said. (This was a large artificial harbor then under federal construction near the mouth of Delaware Bay.) "It will cost several millions of money. Would Pennsylvania ever have constructed it? Certainly never, . . . because it is not for her sole benefit. Would Pennsylvania, New Jersey and Delaware have united to accomplish it at their joint expenses? Certainly not, for the same reason. It could not be done, therefore, but by the general government."

Hayne was right to shrink from the logic of this argument. For its logic does mean that in a rapidly developing economy such as that of America in the eighteenth century, increasing interdependence would bring more and more matters legitimately within the province of the federal government. But logic was not the only aspect of Webster's argument that Hayne was resisting. In the spirit of Hamilton, Webster did perceive the prospect of increasing interdependence and recognized that it could fully realize its promise of wealth and power only with the assistance of the federal government. Moreover, he looked beyond the merely material benefits that such intervention would bring to individuals, classes, and regions toward his grand objective, "the consolidation of the union." This further criterion of the common good could under no circumstances be reconciled with Hayne's "system."

Like Hamilton, Webster sought to make the nation more of a nation. As he conceived this objective, however, he broke from the bleak eighteenth-century realism of Hamilton and turned his imagination toward the vistas of social possibility being opened up by the rising romantic movement of his day. By "consolidation" Webster did not mean merely attachment to the union arising from economic benefits. Indeed, he blamed Hayne for regarding the union "as a mere question of present and temporary expedience; nothing more than a mere matter of profit and loss . . . to be preserved, while it suits local and temporary purposes to preserve it; and to be sundered whenever it shall be found to thwart such purposes."

The language brings to mind the imagery of another romantic nationalist, Edmund Burke; in his famous assault upon the French Revolution and social contract theory, he proclaimed that "the state ought not to be considered as nothing better than a partnership agreement in a trade of pepper and coffee, calico or tobacco, or some other such low concern, to be taken up for a little temporary interest, and to be dissolved at the fancy of the parties," but rather as "a partnership in all science; a partnership in all art; a partnership in every virtue, and in all perfection."

A later formulation echoes Burke's words and phrasing even more exactly, as Webster sets forth the organic conception of the nation: "The Union," he said, "is not a temporary partnership of states. It is an association of people, under a constitution of government, uniting their power, joining together their highest interests, cementing their present enjoyments, and blending into one indivisible mass, all their hopes for the future."

Webster articulated this conception most vividly not in Congress or before the Supreme Court, but at public gatherings on patriotic occasions. There the constraints of a professional and adversarial audience upon his imagination were relaxed and his powers as myth maker released. Consider what some call the finest of his occasional addresses, his speech at the laying of the cornerstone of the Bunker Hill Monument on June 17, 1825. As in his advocacy and in his debates, his theme was the union. What he did, however, was not to make an argument for the union, but to tell a story about it—a story about its past with a lesson for its future.

The plot was simple: how American union foiled the British oppressors in 1775. They had thought to divide and conquer, anticipating that the other colonies would be cowed by the severity of the punishment visited on Massachusetts and that the other seaports would be seduced by the prospect of gain from trade diverted from Boston. "How miserably such reasoners deceived themselves!" exclaimed the orator. "Everywhere the unworthy boon was rejected with scorn. The fortunate occasion was seized, everywhere, to show to the whole world that the Colonies were swayed by no local interest, no partial interest, no selfish interest." In the imagery of Webster, the battle of Bunker Hill was a metaphor of the united people. As Warren, Prescott, Putnam, and Stark had fought side by side; as the four colonies of New England had on that day stood together with "one cause, one country, one heart"; so also "the feeling of resistance . . . possessed the whole American people." So much for Calhoun and his "system."

From this myth of war Webster drew a lesson for peace. "In a day of peace, let us advance the arts of peace and the works of peace. . . . Let us develop the resources of our land, call forth its powers, build up its institutions, and see whether we also, in our day and generation, may not perform something worthy to be remembered." Then he concluded with abrupt and brutal rhetoric: "Let our object be: OUR COUNTRY, OUR WHOLE COUNTRY, AND NOTHING BUT OUR COUNTRY."

With his own matchless sensibility Abraham Lincoln deployed the doctrine and imagery of Webster to animate the North during the Civil War. Lincoln's nationalism, like Webster's, had a positive message for peacetime, and it was this message that set the course of the country's development for the next several generations. Much that he did derived from the original Hamiltonian program, which, long frustrated by the dominance of the compact theory, now burst forth in legislative and executive action. During the war years, not only was slavery given the death blow, but also an integrated program of positive federal involvement was put through in the fields of banking and currency, transportation, the tariff, land grants to homesteaders, and aid to higher education. In the following decades, an enormous expansion of the economy propelled the United States into the age of industrialism, which in due course engendered its typical problems of deprivation, inequality, and class conflict.

A Republican, Theodore Roosevelt, first attempted to cope with these problems in terms of the national idea. Throughout his public career, an associate has written, Roosevelt "kept one steady purpose, the solidarity, the essential unity of our country. . . . All the details of his action, the specific policies he stated, arise from his underlying purpose for the Union." Like other Progressives, Roosevelt was disturbed by the rising conflicts between groups and classes and sought to offset them by timely reform. In this sense integration was T.R.'s guiding aim, and he rightly christened his cause "The New Nationalism." Effective advocacy of this cause, however, fell to another Roosevelt a generation later, when the failings of industrialism were raising far greater dangers to the union.

None of the main points in Franklin Roosevelt's famous inaugural of March 4, 1933, can be summarized without reference to the nation. The emergency is national because of "the interdependence of the various elements in, and parts of, the United States." Our purpose must be, first, "the establishment of a sound national economy," and beyond that "the assurance of a rounded and permanent national life." The mode of action must be national, conducted by the federal government and carried out "on a national scale," helped "by national planning." No other thematic term faintly rivals the term "nation" as noun or adjective, in emphasis. Democracy is mentioned only once in Roosevelt's address; liberty, equality, or the individual not at all.

Franklin Roosevelt's nationalism was threefold. First it was a doctrine of federal centralization, and in his administration, in peace as well as war, the balance of power in the federal system swung sharply toward Washington. Roosevelt called not only for a centralization of government, but also for a nationalization of politics. In these years a new kind of mass politics arose. The old rustic and sectional politics gave way to a new urban and class politics dividing electoral forces on a nationwide basis.

The third aspect of Roosevelt's nationalism was expressed in his policies. Those policies do not make a neat package and include many false starts and failures and ad hoc expedients. Yet in their overall impact one can detect the old purpose of "consolidation of the union."

During the very first phase of the New Deal, based on the National Industrial Recovery Act, this goal was explicit. In its declaration of policy, the act, having declared a "national emergency," called for "cooperative action among trade groups" and "united action of labor and management" under "adequate government sanctions and supervision." Engulfed in red, white, and blue propaganda, the NRA, after a first brief success, failed to achieve that coordinated effort and had virtually collapsed by the time it was declared unconstitutional in 1935. The second New Deal which followed, however, brought about fundamental and lasting changes in the structure of the American government and economy.

The paradox of the second New Deal is that although at the time it was intensely divisive, in the end it enhanced national solidarity. The divisiveness will be readily granted by anyone who remembers the campaign of 1936. The tone was set by Roosevelt's speech accepting the Democratic nomination. In swollen and abrasive hyperbole he promised that, just as 1776 had wiped out "political tyranny," so 1936 would bring "economic tyranny" to an end. The "economic royalist" metaphor that was launched into the political battle by this speech expressed the emerging purpose of the New Deal to create a new balance of power in the economy by means of a series of basic structural reforms. The Wagner Act was the most important and characteristic reform. Utilizing its protections of the right to organize and to bargain collectively, trade unions swept through industry in a massive organizing effort. Despite bitter and sometimes bloody resistance in what can only be called class war, over the years not only practices but also attitudes eventually were altered. The life of the working stiff was never again the same.

The Rooseveltian reforms had two aspects. In their material aspect they brought about a redistribution of power in favor of certain groups. No less important was their symbolic significance as recognition of the full membership of these groups in the national community. Industrial labor and recent immigrants won a degree of acceptance in the national consciousness and in everyday social intercourse that they had not previously enjoyed. In Roosevelt's appointments to the judiciary, Catholics and Jews were recognized as never before. He named the first Italo-American and the first blacks ever appointed to the federal bench. As Joseph Alsop has recently observed, "the essence of his achievement" was that he "included the excluded." And with such high spirits! He once addressed the

Daughters of the American Revolution as "Fellow Immigrants!"

Recently I had a letter from a friend who asked: Did not "the new social democracy, which arose with the New Deal, make popular sacrifice, not least for foreign policy, more difficult to obtain?" Just the opposite, I replied. And I went on to recall how during the war it often occurred to me that we were lucky that those sudden, vast demands being put upon the people in the name of national defense had been preceded by a period of radical national reform. An anecdote will illustrate my point. One hot day in the late summer of 1944 while crossing France we stopped to vote by absentee ballot in the presidential election. "Well, Guthrie," I said to one of the noncoms, "let's line up these men and vote them for Roosevelt." That lighthearted remark was entirely in keeping with the situation. Most of the GIs were from fairly poor families in the Bronx and New Jersey. Politics didn't greatly concern them, but nothing was more natural to them than to vote for the man who had brought WPA, social security, and other benefits to their families. Even among the battalion officers I can think of only two who did not vote for Roosevelt—the colonel and a staff officer from New York City named something or other the fourth.

None of these conflicts in nation building is ever wholly terminated. Sectionalism still flares up from time to time, as between frost belt and sun belt. So also does class struggle. Similarly today, the cleavages among ethnic groups that boiled up with a new bitterness in the 1960s are far from being resolved.

The issue is not just ethnicity, but race. To be sure, ethnic pluralism is a fact—there are said to be ninety-two ethnic groups in the New York area alone—but this broad focus obscures the burning issue, which is the coexistence of blacks and whites in large numbers on both sides. That question of numbers is crucial. In other times and places one can find instances of a small number of one race living in relative peace in a society composed overwhelmingly of the other race. "Tokenism" is viable. But the facts rule out that solution for the United States.

Another option is the model of "separate but equal." In some circumstances this option could be carried out on a decent and democratic basis. It is, for instance, the way the French-speaking citizens of Quebec would like to live in relation to Canada as a whole. And, commonly, Canadians contrast favorably what they call their "mosaic society" with the American "melting pot." But in the present crisis Americans have rejected this option in law and in opinion as segregation. American nationalism demands that diversity be dealt with not by separation, but by integration.

119

For John F. Kennedy and Lyndon Johnson, the question was, first of all, civil rights. This meant securing for blacks the legal and political rights that had been won for whites in other generations. But the problem of civil rights, which was mainly a problem of the South, merged with the problem of black deprivation, which was especially a problem of northern cities. Johnson's "war on poverty" characterized the main thrust of the Great Society measures which he built on the initiatives of Kennedy. To think of these measures as concerned simply with "the poor" is to miss the point. The actual incidence of poverty meant that their main concern would be with the living conditions and opportunities of blacks, and especially those who populated the decaying areas of the great urban centers swollen by migration from the South to the North during and after World War II.

These programs were based on the recognition that membership in one ethnic group rather than another can make a great difference to your life chances. In trying to make the opportunities somewhat less unequal, they sought to bring the individuals belonging to disadvantaged groups—as was often said—"into the mainstream of American life." The rhetoric of one of Johnson's most impassioned speeches echoes this purpose. Only a few days after a civil rights march led by Martin Luther King had been broken up by state troopers in full view of national television, he introduced the Voting Rights Act of 1965 into Congress. Calling upon the myths of former wars, like other nationalist orators before him, he harked back to Lexington and Concord and to Appomattox in his summons to national effort. "What happened in Selma," he continued, "is part of a larger movement which reaches into every section and state of America. It is the effort of American Negroes to secure for themselves the full blessings of American life. . . ." Then, declaring that "their cause must be our cause too," he closed with solemn echo of the song of the marchers: *"And—we—shall—overcome."*

Considering where we started from some thirty years ago, our progress has been substantial. Still, few will assert that our statecraft—from poverty programs to affirmative action to busing—has been adequate to the objective. This problem still awaits its Alexander Hamilton. We may take some comfort from the fact that it is continuous with his great work. The Founders confronted the task of founding a nation-state. Our present exercise in nation building is no less challenging. What we are attempting has never before been attempted by any country at any time. It is to create within a liberal, democratic framework a society in which vast numbers of both black and white people live in free and equal intercourse—political, economic, and social. It is a unique, a stupendous, demand, but the national idea will let us be satisfied with nothing less.

The federal system that confronts Ronald Reagan is the outcome of these three great waves of centralization: the Lincolnian, the Rooseveltian, and the Johnsonian. By means of his new federalism President Reagan seeks radically to decentralize that system. Does the history of the national idea in American politics suggest any criticism or guidance?

I hope, at least, that it does something to undermine the appeal of compact theory rhetoric. Rhetoric is important. Words are the means through which politicians reach the motivations of voters and by which leaders may shape those motivations. Both the compact theory and the national theory touch nerves of the body politic. Each conveys a very different sense of nationhood—or the lack thereof. My theme has been the national theory, which envisions one people, at once sovereign and subject, source of authority and substance of history, asserting, through conflict and in diversity, our unity of origin and of destiny.

Such an image does not yield a rule for allocating functions between levels of government. That is for practical men, assisted no doubt by the policy sciences. But the imagery of the national idea can prepare the minds of practical men to recognize in the facts of our time the call for renewed effort to consolidate the union. The vice of the compact theory is that it obscures this issue, diverts attention from the facts, and muffles the call for action.

Today this issue is real. A destructive pluralism—sectional, economic, and ethnic—disrupts our common life. It is foolish to use the rhetoric of political discourse to divert attention from that fact. I would ask the new federalists not only to give up their diversionary rhetoric, but positively to advocate the national idea. This does not mean they must give up federal reform. A nationalist need not always be a centralizer. For philosophical and for pragmatic reasons he may prefer a less active federal government. The important thing is to keep alive in our speech and our intentions the move toward the consolidation of the union. People will differ on what and how much needs to be done. The common goal should not be denied. We may need a new federalism. We surely need a new nationalism. I plead with the new federalists: come out from behind that Jeffersonian verbiage, and take up the good old Hamiltonian cause.

7

Federalism and Civic Virtue: The Antifederalists and the Constitution

Gary L. McDowell

When the delegates to the Federal Convention gathered in Philadelphia in May 1787, they were obliged to bring with them a good bit of political baggage. They were, after all, convening to reform an existing scheme of governance, the Articles of Confederation. The very presence of the articles was a nearly insurmountable obstacle to those who would blatantly seek to discard that document and begin anew, for the articles signified the political legitimacy of thirteen sovereign states.

The states had come into being at different times and under different circumstances. They had cooperated when necessary to throw off what a majority of the citizens had come to see as the yoke of English tyranny, they had cooperated again to form a confederation to meet certain common exigencies, and here they were cooperating yet again to reform the confederation. The states had a history; they had a claim to sovereignty.

With such a history it was inevitable that any effort during the deliberations of the convention to curtail the states' claims to sovereignty would be met with firm resistance. The questions that dominated the work of the convention were not so much about what powers a government properly ought to possess as about which was the proper government to possess them. The discussions and debates in Philadelphia can be understood on one level, then, as a simple struggle over the distribution, or redistribution, of political power.

To the men who argued so eloquently in behalf of nationalism—most notably James Madison, James Wilson, Alexander Hamilton, and Gouverneur Morris—the problem of the Articles of Confederation was nothing less than the theory of government they embraced.

The articles failed to meet the exigencies of the union not because they were not true to their animating principle, confederalism or federalism, but because they were. As Martin Diamond put it, the problem facing the nationalists was to show "not how to be federal in a better way, but how to be better by being less federal."[1] When Madison boasted in *The Federalist* of having found a republican cure for the diseases most incident to republican government through a "judicious modification . . . of the federal principle," he meant *modification*.[2]

Against Madison and his allies, men such as George Mason, Patrick Henry, Melancton Smith, and Richard Henry Lee stood steadfastly opposed. The modification of the federal principle, they thought, had been anything but judicious. Behind the weak polemical concessions of some of the Federalist writers toward confederalism, the Antifederalists saw an awesome concentration of powers all tending toward the same end: the complete dissolution of the states into one simple, consolidated republic. Certainly consolidation would not result immediately from the proposed constitution; the nationalists were too shrewd for that, and the attachment of too many people to confederal principles was too strong. What the Antifederalists fearfully pointed to was the *tendency* of the Constitution toward consolidation. "Ere too many years have passed," Richard Henry Lee cautioned, "we shall see a government far different than a free one" evolve from the new constitution. It would be, he said, "replete with power, danger, and hydra-headed mischief" and would eventually snuff out the lamp of liberty the revolutionary generation had fought so hard to light.[3]

As Jean Yarbrough argues elsewhere in this volume, a look into the literature of the founding period for a theoretical defense of the notion of federalism embraced by the Constitution is in vain. There was no comprehensive defense; even in the celebrated *Federalist*, Publius was content to leave the discussion at the level of "partly federal and partly national." Thus, the Federalists argued against the old understanding of confederalism while the Antifederalists argued for it. No one really argued for the new formulation *as a principle*. To the founding generation, the new version was merely a hybrid, a pragmatic compromise between the two old and warring principles of confederalism and nationalism. And the compromise of two old principles did not necessarily a new principle make. In short, the Constitution was as national as the Federalists could make it and as confederal as the Antifederalists could keep it.

Then, as now, however, political debates that seem to be nothing more than a rhetorical struggle over where political power is to be

123

lodged are often deeper than they first appear. Beneath the important political question of who shall exercise power, today as in 1787, lies a more profound, more interesting, and more important philosophical question: what kind of nation shall we be, what sort of people shall we be?

In order to appreciate the philosophical significance of the debate over federalism, at the outset we must discount Publius's well-known and seemingly authoritative claim that those who argued for confederalism and against the Constitution did so primarily out of the "obvious interest" they had in resisting "all changes which may hazard a diminution of the power, emolument, and consequence of the offices they hold under the state establishments"; or that they had been seduced by the "fairer prospects" of personal elevation they would enjoy "from the subdivision of the empire into several partial confederacies than from its union under one government."[4] The Antifederalists were not merely men who thought it better to be big fish in small ponds; among the ranks of the Antifederalists were men whose names and national reputations dwarfed those of many of the leading Federalists such as Madison and Hamilton. The debate involved far more than the political self-interest of the parties; it was a fundamental debate over how best to structure the new government in order to render political power safe to individual liberty. To view the debate in any other light is to lose the significance that the principle of confederalism had for the Founders.

The basic Antifederalist argument was that by strengthening too greatly the federal *authority*, the new constitution had seriously undermined the federal *principle*.[5] Yet most Antifederalists were not completely opposed to a movement toward a stronger union; nor were all Federalists completely dedicated, or even primarily dedicated, to a completely consolidated union.[6] As Federalist Fisher Ames put it,

> Too much provision cannot be made against a consolidation. The state governments represent the wishes and feelings, and local interests of the people. They are the safeguard and ornament of the Constitution; they will protract the period of our liberties; they will afford a shelter against the abuse of power, and will be the natural avengers of our violated rights.[7]

Thus the difference between the Federalists and the Antifederalists on this issue (like most others) was not a matter of black and white; there was a vast area of gray.[8]

What Kind of People? What Kind of Nation?

The Antifederalists were not simple-minded agrarians who longed for a regime of pastoral simplicity; nor were they intemperate utopians who thought they might create "an empire of perfect wisdom and perfect virtue."[9] They were far more modern and far more modest in their claims. Like the Federalists, the Antifederalists were modern liberals who believed that the only legitimate end of government was liberty; and their concern for developing civic virtue was an "instrumental" concern. In their theoretical scheme, political liberty was the end, and civic virtue was one of the necessary means for achieving it. In a sense, the Antifederalists and the Federalists display the two sides of the coin of modern liberalism. The Antifederalists and the Federalists alike were "committed to both union and the states; to both the great American republic and the small self-governing community; to both commerce and civic virtue; to both private gain and public good."[10] They differed from one another, however, in the emphasis each placed on the different sides of the liberal political tradition that had been received in America. While the Federalists argued forcefully for the necessity of the union, the great or extensive republic, the virtues of commerce, and the power of private gain to promote the public good, the Antifederalists endeavored to defend the role of the states as small self-governing communities, the necessity of some kind of civic virtue, and the notion that the public good is more than simply the sum of private gains.

On the whole, the Federalists believed that the great "empire of commerce" they envisioned would give practical effect to the belief that each man is endowed by his creator with the inalienable right to pursue his happiness. Commerce, they thought, would destroy the social castes created by ancient conventions such as hereditary claims and replace them with more natural distinctions. A commercial republic would allow the best and the brightest to exercise their natural talents to the fullest, unencumbered by rigid social distinctions. The commercial spirit when unleashed would thus elevate the natural *aristoi* to heights never before imagined. Furthermore, by making commerce the dominant vocation of a free people, that people would develop what Martin Diamond called the "bourgeois virtues"—honesty, punctuality, thrift, and decency. While the bourgeois virtues may lack the luster of virtue proper, a people characterized by such habits would prove to be a morally decent and politically stable people. Thus the purpose of any sound constitution was to encourage and regulate commerce, not suppress it. There would be a sort of civic virtue to be had from the everyday and ordinary activities of a people engaged in commerce and pursuit of their self-interest. The Antifederalists, though, did not believe this to be sufficient.

The Antifederalists' reservations about the Constitution were, in the end, reservations precisely about the Federalists' faith in an extensive commercial republic with a multiplicity of hustling and bustling interests. The Antifederalists maintained that the Constitution (and the nation it envisioned) rested on nothing more than a misguided reliance on the power of naked and unashamed self-interest to promote the common good. In the Antifederalists' science of politics, that would not do. The disjunction between the self and society was too great to be left unattended.

The Antifederalists' doubts about the institutional structures of the Constitution, especially its feeble nod toward federalism, reflected their deeper doubts about the kind of polity such a constitution would spawn, and whether such a polity could remain free and republican. The underlying (and largely unifying) sentiment that characterized Antifederalism was the belief that a "community of mere interest" was insufficient to secure safe republican government and political liberty. The Antifederalists believed that "the American polity had to be a moral community if it was to be anything, and they saw that the seat of that community must be in the hearts of the people."[11] For the Antifederalists, political liberty and civic virtue were inseparable; and it was this maxim they thought the Federalists had abandoned in their rash modification of the federal principle in their new constitution.

Commerce, despite the good it brought, carried with it a dangerous spirit—a spirit that could enervate the "manly virtues" of a republican people, a spirit that could cause people to turn away from one another and bury themselves in their own narrow, banal interests, a spirit that could result in an estrangement between the people and the polity. To guard against these dangerous propensities, the Antifederalists urged the maintenance of the states with sovereignty sufficient to be truly self-governing communities. The Antifederalists saw the small republic as the way through which America must pass in order to secure free government.

The maintenance of a confederation of small republics, the Antifederalists insisted, would achieve three things essential to free government that would be missing in the Federalists' extended commercial republic.[12] First, by being closer to the people, the small republic would serve to "create a confidence in, and a respect for the laws; and thereby induce the sensible and virtuous part of the community to declare in favor of the laws and to support them without . . . military force."[13] Second, in small republics the government would be more responsive and responsible to the people because there would be a greater homogeneity among the citizens. This would engender a greater coincidence of interests between the representative and the represented. The third and most important advantage for free government to be expected from a small republic was its greater ability to mold the manners and the morals of the people. The Antifederalists were far more concerned than the Federalists with the *kind* of citizens that would fill the republic. A small republic, the Antifederalists' faith held, would inculcate the kind of civic virtue peculiarly essential to republican government. Each of these tenets of Antifederalism needs to be fleshed out in order to understand the passionate commitment of the Antifederalists to confederalism.

The Voluntary Attachment of the People to the Polity. A permanent problem of politics is how to make the people obey the laws of the polity. In other words, how does a constitution transform human beings into citizens? The crux of the problem for republican governments, in the view of both the Antifederalists and the Federalists, was how to foster a voluntary attachment of the people to the polity. The general consensus was that, throughout the political history of mankind, all governments operated on one of two principles. "The important springs which alone move the machines and give them their intended influence and control," argued the *Federal Farmer*, "are force and persuasion: by the former men are compelled, by the latter they are drawn." In the Antifederal science of politics the object was to "arm persuasion on every side, and to render force as little necessary as possible."[14]

The Antifederalists believed that the true foundation of public trust and confidence and public morality was intimate government. A confederation of relatively small, self-governing states was necessary so that public "opinion founded on the knowledge of those who govern, procures obedience without force."[15] It was this understanding that came into direct conflict with the Federalists, who believed generally that the best political foundation for such public virtues was *effective* government, not *intimate* government.[16]

The Antifederalist argument was that for governments to draw unto themselves the public veneration necessary for stable and orderly governance, they had to provide the citizenry with an opportunity for involvement. Good administration was not enough; it had to be a kind of participatory administration. And this could be had only in republics of limited extent. To the Antifederalists, effective government as pushed by the Federalists might inspire a kind of superficial confidence in the people, but in time it would only serve to sap their

127

confidence in their ability to be truly self-governing.

Effective government that demanded nothing of the citizen by way of active involvement would foster an unhealthy dependence among the people on the government. Under such an arrangement, the people would neglect participation in public affairs, and would therefore cease to be self-governing.[17] As "long as the people are free," the *Federal Farmer* warned, "they will preserve free governments; [but] when they become tired of freedom, arbitrary government must take place."[18]

The true foundation of individual liberty, in the opinion of most Antifederal writers, lay in a structure of government that demanded a more immediate involvement in the political affairs of the community. The extensive commercial republic preferred by the Federalists would deny that opportunity for civic participation. Encouraged to pursue their narrow, selfish inclinations uninterrupted by public demands, the people would soon find themselves incapable of self-government; they would, rather, find themselves under a tyranny of clerks and accountants—or, worse, under the boot of a standing army.

It was a common article of the Antifederal faith that large republics, especially one as extensive as that envisioned by the Federalists, could secure public obedience only through a standing army to bring the public force down on the citizens and make them do their duties.[19] A strong military establishment was, therefore, the first step toward despotism. The solution to this threat was simple: replace a standing army over a large republic with militias drawn from the several small, confederated republics. This was not only desirable, it was possible. In a small republic, as we have seen, there would be the public affection necessary to support the laws because the laws would be adapted to the manners of the people rather than the manners of the people being made to conform to the laws by force.[20] There would thus be no need for force—"the parent and support of tyranny"[21]—in a small republic.

Reliance on the state militia was useful for other reasons as well. A militia, like jury trials, was a most effective means of drawing the citizenry into the conduct of public affairs in a very immediate way. Such public service would foster that necessary sense of attachment between the citizen and his community.[22] Service would give them a stake in their republic; they would care more because they had given a measure of themselves. The citizen would be a part of the community; the community a part of the citizen.

With such a public attachment to the public interest, the task of representation would then be a rather simple matter. In a small republic of a markedly homogeneous population, the representative would be cut from the same cloth as the represented and would have a stronger attachment to the opinions, passions, and interests of his constituents.

The Genuine Responsibility of the Government to the Governed. The basic question facing those dedicated to creating a representative form of government is how closely the governors should reflect the will of the governed. To the Federalists, the answer was "not completely." The friends of the Constitution saw a definite advantage in a scheme of representation that put some distance between the governed and the governors. They saw no grave danger in a system that sought to "refine and enlarge the public views" rather than simply register them. It was even possible, probably likely, as Publius suggested, that occasions would arise when "the public voice pronounced by the representatives of the people, will be more consonant to the public good, than if pronounced by the people themselves convened for the purpose."[23]

The Antifederalists could not accept this novel arrangement. Any system of successive filtrations, as James Madison called them, meant too great a gulf between public opinion and public policy. In the Antifederal way of looking at things, popular government meant a government dominated and controlled by popular opinion; and this meant the government had to be tied, as closely as possible, to the people. Any institutional devices that widened the gap between governors and governed, that encouraged a kind of freewheeling discretion on the part of the rulers, suffered in being less democratic than truly popular government must be. Remote government was dangerous government. When they examined the Federalists' handiwork in the new constitution, the Antifederalists saw this cardinal principle of republican government seriously weakened. Even the most representative body, the House of Representatives, provided a "mere shred or rag of representation."[24] The defect of a regime of insufficient representation was that government would likely "fall into the hands of the few and the great."[25]

The Antifederalists were not unaware of the problems that had existed within the states during the confederal period. While they generally rejected the Federalist claim that it was a "critical period," they had to admit that there had been circumstances in which a factious spirit had "tainted" the public administration of the states. The catalogue of defects Madison put forth in *The Federalist*—"a rage for paper money, for an abolition of debts, for an equal distribution of property"—were facts with which the Antifederalists had to reckon.[26]

The immediate danger to the Antifederalists, though, was the underhanded political use to which these abuses were being put. By charging the abuses to the "democratic part of the community," the "aristocratical men" had created the pretext for urging a radical change in the forms of government. Whatever the diseases had been, the Antifederalists were convinced that the Federalist remedy was even more toxic. As Richard Henry Lee glibly put it, "To say . . . that a bad government ought to be established for fear of anarchy, is really saying that we must kill ourselves for fear of dying."[27]

In a properly constructed republic, representatives "should be a true picture of the people; possess the knowledge of their circumstances and their wants; sympathize in all their distresses and be disposed to seek their true interests."[28] To secure this happy state, the Antifederal logic ran, it was essential to raise the number of representatives to such a number as to allow the assembly to hold the same inclinations, opinions, passions, and interests as "the people themselves would were they all assembled."[29] It was this desire for sameness between ruler and ruled that formed the core of the Antifederal theory of representation.[30]

Plain honesty and common sense in elected officials were the only requisites to sound representative government. Not only were the best and the brightest of the community not essential, they might even prove (some Antifederalists argued that they definitely would prove) to be a danger. It was more important that morally sturdy men of common interests and residence represent one another: equal men governing their equals equally. The most sensible of the Antifederalists, however, had to concede that whatever its merits in theory, in practice a strict sameness between the representative and his constituents was not possible. Given this practical difficulty, the Antifederalists were willing to settle for a scheme of representation that they deemed sufficiently large so as to allow all orders of the community access.

A numerous legislative body would not be captured by the great and the mighty, by the aristocratic portion of the community. If a strict sameness could not be arranged, then it was desirable at least to have the representative body be "composed principally of respectable yeomanry," what we would call the middle or working class. The reason was simple. This broadly based representation of the middle class would lead to a greater likelihood that the public interest would be pursued, because "the interest of both the rich and the poor are involved in that of the middling class."[31]

The Antifederalists had an alternative to the Federalists' niggardly proposal for representation: first, the representation of the first branch of the national legislature should be as full as circumstances would permit; second, and most important, "as much power as possible [should be left] in the states where genuine responsibility could exist."[32] "It is impracticable in this extensive country," the *Federal Farmer* argued, "to have a federal representation sufficiently democratic or substantially drawn from the body of the people."[33] The most obvious solution was to maintain the primacy of the states where it would be possible for the legislatures to be "so numerous as almost to be the people themselves."[34] Only under a confederate form would the government be rendered properly responsive and truly responsible to the people.

The Moral Development of the Citizenry. In a sense the advantages the Antifederalists saw in fostering a voluntary attachment of the people to the polity and in securing a genuinely responsible representation derived from the third and most important quality of small republicanism: it permitted the cultivation of a certain public morality. For if the republic properly shaped the sensibilities of the citizenry, then popular affection for the regime and the coincidence of interest between the representative and the represented would not prove too difficult to secure. Recognizing that "government operates upon the spirit of the people, as well as the spirit of the people operating upon it," the Antifederalists were dedicated to a republican form of government that would produce republican citizens, to a form of republican government that would be able to mold the manners and morals of the people in such a way as to render them morally compatible with the political demands of republican government.[35]

It was not simply that the "manners, sentiments, and interests of the people should be similar," though that was surely to be desired. What was more important was that the shared sentiments be of a certain kind.[36] Special care had to be taken in forming the constitution of any government because the opinions and the manners of human beings are mutable.[37] The institutional forms of a government will determine, to a great extent, the form and substance of the habits and manners of the people. What was required was a constitutional scheme that would promote the kind of public virtues peculiarly necessary in a republic. In particular, what was demanded, the Antifederalists thought, was a kind of civic virtue or public-spiritedness that would produce citizens willing and able to "wade up to their knees in blood, to defend their governments" and sturdy enough morally to resist the stultifying "voluptuousness" of wealth and prosperity.[38]

"As the people become more luxurious," Charles Turner told the Massachusetts Ratifying Convention, "they become more incapacitated of governing themselves." The progress of commerce begets such luxury that there is a danger of moral decay. With the unleashing of commercial vices—pride, ambition, envy, and lust for power—there would come a diminution of the spirit of patriotism and the commitment to community justice.[39] Such commercial luxury was "the parent of inequality, the foe to virtue, and the enemy to restraint." The dilemma posed by this state of affairs, the perspicacious *Cato* observed, is that the government will in turn "assimilate the manners and opinions of the community to it."[40]

It was this corruption of the human spirit born of luxury that the Antifederalists considered the tragic disease of all commercial republics and especially of the one proposed and defended by the Federalists. The "want of public virtue, in preferring private interest to every other consideration" was the disease civic virtue in small republics was in the main designed to treat, if not cure.[41] In the midst of luxury it is easy to choose comfort and convenience over the constant vigilance liberty demands. Thus, in the midst of a free and comfortable people there can arise a most brutal tyranny, not by the hand of a forceful conqueror but from the indifference of a feeble national character. It was for this reason that the Antifederalists declaimed against the Constitution as being morally indifferent.

This concern over the potentially destructive relationship between commerce and virtue lay at the heart of the Antifederalist demand for small republics conducive to civic virtue. To dig a bit more deeply into this theoretical concern, however, we must move behind the polemical and therefore somewhat superficial Antifederalist writings to the older tradition of political thinking that the Antifederalist persuasion itself reflected.[42]

The tradition of political writing that formed the backdrop of the American founding was rich and varied; from Coke to Blackstone, Hobbes to Locke, Machiavelli to Harrington, the founding generation pored over the books, tracts, and pamphlets of early modernity. As the seventeenth century faded into the eighteenth, writers began to address and attempt to resolve the difficulties implicit in the new teachings of commercial republicanism. They sought to effect a synthesis of the modern notions of polity and economy that had come to dominate political thinking. During the mid-eighteenth century the greatest burst of creative energy was to be found in Scotland. Thus the Scottish Enlightenment has been aptly described as a period of "remarkable efflorescence."[43] And it was there, in Glasgow and Edinburgh, that close attention was given to the often troubling relationship between wealth and virtue.[44]

The writers of the Scottish School proved to be an important resource to the republicans across the Atlantic who were beginning to work their way through the theoretical jungle of political economy. Dedicated to forming free governments within the existing context of commercial enterprise, the American founding generation sought to create a nation that would rest on the most solid theoretical foundation. Cautious theorizing rooted in experience characterized the work of the Scots; and in that body of work both the Federalists and the Antifederalists found support for their divergent schemes of how best to weld the modern notions of polity and economy to fit the particular circumstances of America.

Adam Ferguson, along with his fellow countrymen Adam Smith, John Miller, and others (but not Hume),

> . . . took a long cool look at both sides of the medal of modern civilization, and what they saw was the paradox of commerce and manufactures giving rise on the one hand to personal liberty and security, the blessings of the rule of law, but at the same time and equally inevitably producing a second-rate sort of society full of second-rate citizens pursuing comparatively worthless objects.[45]

Thus, if David Hume is the father of much of the Federalists' confidence in their extended commercial republic (as Douglass Adair suggested so long ago), then other Scots like Ferguson may well stand behind the reservations and doubts about the system voiced by the Antifederalists.[46] Ferguson's *Essay on the History of Civil Society* is a valuable source for understanding many of the arguments inherent in the Antifederalist position.

Ferguson was not pusillanimous in his warning about the tragedy of modernity:

> Men frequently, while they study to improve their fortunes, neglect themselves; and while they reason for their country, forget the considerations that most deserve their attention. Numbers, riches, and other resources of war, are highly important: but nations consist of men; and a nation consisting of degenerate and cowardly men, is weak; a nation consisting of vigorous, public-spirited, and resolute men, is strong. The resources of war, where other advantages are equal, may decide a contest; but the resources of war, in hands that cannot employ them, are of no avail.[47]

Ferguson's deepest lesson is that history is not cyclical; nor is progress or decline simply inevitable. The decisive factor in determining whether a nation will survive and prosper in freedom or decline into despotism is not its wealth or refinement; it is the character of its citizens. In establishing political institutions, the prudent statesman must look to human nature and take his bearings from both the virtues and the vices of the human economy, because "schemes of perfect corruption are at least as impracticable as schemes of perfect virtue."[48]

The problem Ferguson saw in commercial society is not simply commerce or the objects of commerce, it is the influence of the commercial spirit on the attitude of the populace. The laws of a commercial society, according to Ferguson, must look to preserving liberty. For man, if left free, will apply himself according to the dictates of his interest and his natural abilities. "Commerce . . . is the branch in which men committed to the effects of their own experience are least apt to go wrong." The object of policy is to protect the liberty necessary for man to pursue the objects of his industry and desire. The commercially active citizen when pursuing his own interest, Ferguson believed, really does more for the common good than if he "forget[s] his own interest to lay plans for his country." The wise statesman will "protect the industrious in the pursuit of his occupation. . . . If a protection be required, it must be granted; if crimes and frauds be committed, they must be repressed; and government can pretend to do no more." But the constitution must look beyond merely designing institutions with the teeth to secure the "person and property of the subject." To secure true liberty, the constitution must seek to develop the political character of the citizens.[49]

Commercial societies, however, bring with them the danger of corruption of the human spirit. Commercial nations tend to introduce wealth "unsupported by personal elevation and virtues, as the great foundation of distinction." No longer concerned with such things as magnanimity, courage, or the love of mankind, men in such a society grow "either rapacious, deceitful, and violent, ready to trespass on the rights of others; or servile, mercenary, and base, prepared to relinquish their own."[50] The constitution of such a commercial society must encourage men to do more than pursue their selfish interests, at the same time that it secures the liberty essential to such self-interested pursuits. Ferguson's solution was a simple political one. A constitution will be able to cultivate the political character of the citizen to the degree that it admits him "by representation or otherwise to an actual share of the [government]." By giving men the responsibility for conducting their civil affairs, the constitution provides them with the opportunity of exercising their best talents. And it is in the activity of politics that civic virtue of the sort the Antifederalists demanded is born.[51]

In the vigorous give-and-take of political life, men are inevitably called upon to look beyond the narrow limits of home and hearth to the broader concerns of their commonwealth. Through deliberation and discussion of public affairs, men are drawn outside the small circle of their most selfish inclinations, in spite of themselves. Civic virtue develops from the activity of politics not because man is disposed to regard the public interest as the end of his conduct; civic virtue , rather, is cultivated because in pressing the claims of his own interest, each man is forced into community with other individuals with the same mission.

Politics, then, encourages a kind of spirited self-reliance. It demands, above all else, that a people *think* about the public interest and how a certain view of the public interest may better serve one's private interest. But such a politics also encourages a kind of communal dialogue and an appreciation for the necessity of compromise. Through the act of politics wherein each proves his own interest, the individual is pulled closer both to his fellows and to his polity. The necessary welding of man to man, and of citizen to country, depends upon the kinds of institutional arrangements a constitution provides.

It is crucial to Ferguson's liberalism and the republicanism of the Antifederalists that the people be drawn into the conduct of their affairs. For not only does participation help overcome the isolating tendency of modern society, but also it generates a feeling of attachment to the laws the people must obey. Such an arrangement of active participation fuses to the legal pronouncements a veneration that results in a jealous attachment to the legal order. And of all the constitutional arrangements that can be designed to accomplish this, one thing is certain: public-spiritedness is far more easily cultivated in a small republic than in a large one.

Great empires, Ferguson thought, are exposed to dangers and disorders that will in time demand military force to keep order. Indeed, Ferguson was convinced that among "the circumstances . . . which in the event of national prosperity, and in the result of commercial arts, lead to the establishment of despotism, there is none, perhaps, that arrives at this termination, with so sure an aim, as the perpetual enlargement of territory." Echoing somewhat his teacher Montesquieu and foreshadowing Tocqueville, Ferguson went to the heart of the matter:

> Small communities, however corrupted, are not prepared for despotical government: their members, crouded together, and contiguous to the seats of power, never forget their relation to the public; they pry, with habits of familiarity and freedom, into the pretensions of those who would rule; and

where the love of equality, and the sense of justice, have failed, they act on motives of faction, emulation, and envy. . . . In proportion as territory is extended, its parts lose their relative importance to the whole. Its inhabitants cease to perceive their connection with the state, and are seldom united in the execution of any national, or even of any factious, designs. Distance from the seats of administration and indifference to the persons who contend for preferment, teach the majority to consider themselves as the subjects of a sovereignty, not as members of a political body. It is remarkable that enlargement of territory, by rendering the individual of less consequence to the public, and less able to intrude with his counsel . . . tends to diminish the numbers who are consulted in legislation or in other matters of government.[52]

The result of such a polity is that in time the "statesman and the warrior" are replaced in the conduct of political affairs by "the mere clerk and accountant." The government becomes, as Tocqueville embellished the thought, a benevolent shepherd and the people nothing more than a timid and hard-working flock of sheep. A constitution that glorifies the commercial arts within the context of a large and potentially remote republic and that does nothing to create a countervailing force whereby to form the "apprehensions and the habits" of the people, is a constitution with critical flaws. The lessons of Ferguson and of other theorists of similar persuasion, whose works were the standard reading fare of the times, were not lost on the Antifederalists as they waged their rhetorical battle against the Federalists in the name of what they understood to be true republicanism.[53]

In considering these three things most conducive to free, stable republican government—popular attachment to the polity, a government truly responsible to the governed, and a proper public morality—the Antifederalists were convinced that only in a confederation not too dissimilar from the sort established by the Articles of Confederation could they be achieved. The *Farmer* from Pennsylvania captured better than most Antifederalists the crux of the problem and the potential solution. "The peculiar advantages and distinctive properties of a federal republic," he said, summing up the Antifederal position,

are, that each state or member of the confederation may be fully adequate for every local purpose, that it may subsist in a small territory, that the people may have a common interest, possess a competent knowledge of the resources and expenditures of their own particular government, that their immediate representatives and the state governments will know and be known by the citizens, will have a common interest with them, and must bear a part of all the burdens which they may lay upon the people, that they will be responsible to the people, and may be dismissed by them at pleasure; that therefore the government would be a government of confidence and possess sufficient energy without the aid of standing armies.[54]

The purpose of the Antifederalists' demands, it must be remembered, was not state sovereignty for its own sake; their motive was to achieve the best possible government for America. In their estimation, the states were the best instruments for that task. The Antifederalists were wedded to good republican government: everything else was a means to that end.

The Antifederalists were not blind to the problems of corruption that had plagued many of the states under the confederation. They rejected Madison's argument, however, that the tainted administrations of the states under the articles amounted to an indictment of small republicanism generally. They bristled at Madison's and other Federalists' suggestions that small states could never promote the kinds of virtues essential to republican government. When the Federalists argued that small territories of homogeneous populations were the cause not of civic *virtue* but of civic *vice*—majority tyranny—the Antifederalists offered a resounding denial. They tended to agree with Richard Henry Lee's view that their "present discontent" was more the result of "vicious manners, than mistakes in form."[55] The Federalists' confidence in so novel an experiment as the extensive republic comprised of a multiplicity of clashing interests was nearly unbelievable; both theory and history backed the Antifederalists' claim in behalf of confederalism. What the Federalists offered, they believed, were not so much cogent arguments as hopeful assertions.

To cure the republican ills, according to the Antifederalists, the first task was not to abandon the old and trusted forms of confederalism but to restructure and refine those forms to meet the exigencies the articles could not meet. The solution was not to establish a morally indifferent large republic but to bolster the moral forces of the several small republics. Tighten the confederation in the direction of union if need be, they seemed to suggest, but the confederation should remain the rubric under which American politics was to be played out.

The problem of corruption was not a problem unique to small

137

republics, the Antifederalists believed; it was the inevitable concomitant of *any* government. And this much the Antifederalists knew to be true: political corruption would be less likely in a small republic of public-spirited citizens; and when and where it did occur, it would be easier to detect and to remedy in a small republic than in a large one. Intimate government would mean a more decent government.

The Constitution: "A Republican Remedy"

When the Constitution emerged from the secret deliberations of the Federal Convention, the Federalists were able to hit the ground running, with a proposed constitution to defend and promote concretely. Their first burst caught by surprise many of those wary of the new constitution; the Federalists largely reduced the Antifederal opposition to attempts to reconcile contradictions, as Alexander Hamilton snidely commented. In their own loosely organized and theoretically scattered way, though, the Antifederalists were still able to mount a principled attack against the proposed government. Their most famous success, of course, was winning the Federalists' acquiescence in their demand that a bill of rights be added to the Constitution. The Antifederalists exposed other chinks in the Federalist armor, as well, however. History confirms that the Antifederalists' *Brutus* and the *Federal Farmer* voiced warnings about the nature and tendency of the judicial power created by the Constitution that were perhaps even more insightful—and certainly more prophetic—than was Publius in the celebrated defense of that branch in *The Federalist*. Moreover, experience suggests that the pervasive Antifederalist fear that in time the national government would, as George Mason graphically put it, "devour" the states and push the half-hearted federal structure of the Constitution the rest of the way toward one simple consolidated government was not simply wrong.

However insightful and prophetic time has shown the Antifederalists to have been on certain points, of course, their fears on most particulars of the Constitution never came true. On the whole, the constitutional arrangements so eloquently defended in *The Federalist* did turn out as the Federalists promised. The Constitution seems to have succeeded admirably in providing a "republican remedy for the diseases most incident to republican government."

Yet there was something beneath the Antifederalists' institutional concerns that did not die with the ratification of the Constitution; their theoretical reservations have remained very much a part of the principles and traditions of American political life. And in confronting the question of how federal *is* the Constitution, we must confront, as

Jean Yarbrough points out in this volume, what the framers knew to be the more crucial question: how federal *should* the Constitution be? At this deeper level, the Antifederalists are still of great value to us. Their arguments in behalf of the small republic help us today to recognize and minimize whatever defects are inherent in the extensive republic the Federalists established. As Herbert Storing has argued, "Cognizance of the advantages of the small republic may be helpful in avoiding the worst disadvantages of a large one."[56] At least since the time of John Marshall's controversial decision in *McCulloch v. Maryland* supporting national power at the expense of state power, the line of American federalism, running as it does as a fuzzy borderline between the principles of confederalism and nationalism, has been a constant source of controversy in American politics.[57] When things seem too state oriented, the pull of nationalism draws things back to center; similarly, when things veer sharply toward nationalism, the old Antifederal principles of confederalism can serve to put things back on course. In short, the reasons the Antifederalists had for defending their science of confederal politics still have weight.

There are two reasons for reducing the size and the scope of the federal government. First, a government that attempts to do everything will, in the end, not do anything very well. As Tocqueville noted:

A central power, however enlightened, and wise one imagines it to be, can never alone see to all the details of the life of a great nation. It cannot do so because such a task exceeds human strength. When it attempts unaided to create and operate so much complicated machinery, it must be satisfied with very imperfect results or exhaust itself in futile efforts.[58]

The second reason for reducing the grasp and strength of the federal authority is that such a reduction will generate a greater vitality among the people. Decentralization invigorates the people, suffuses the entire society with an orderly but constant motion. In sum, it drives the wheels of imagination and social progress. For although the government may be more efficient or successful in providing for the general welfare, "in the long run the sum of all private undertakings far surpasses anything the government might have done."[59]

Thus the deepest problem posed by big, intrusive government is neither administrative inefficiency nor budgetary bloat; the real problem of big government lies in what it does to us as human beings. The bigger the government, the more remote it will be and the greater the estrangement between the people and the polity. The people will cease to feel much a part of public affairs; they will come to consider themselves, as Ferguson said, more as the subjects of a sovereignty than as members of a political community. With such an estrangement comes a sagging of the spirit: why care about public affairs if the flow of our opinions, passions, and interests is cut off by a government too large to be responsive? The weakening of responsiveness leads ultimately to a diminution of responsibility; and, with that, estrangement becomes divorce.

The importance of American federalism derives from its ability to thwart such a decline. By leaving certain areas of public policy to the states and local communities, federalism forces us to be self-governing. That is not to say that it is easy or enjoyable; the beauty of self-government is in the *opportunity* to exercise our faculties, we should remember, even though the exercise itself may be frustrating and annoying. In the activity of politics, demanded as it is by federalism, is to be found the cure for what Tocqueville called administrative despotism; the best safeguard against a government of "drones and placemen," as Richard Henry Lee described it. Through federalism, with its reliance on voluntary associations and local effort, will come good popular government of citizens rather than a government by clerks.

Conclusion

By decentralizing the administration of the national government, we will shift responsibility back to the states and localities for the services it is thought the government should provide, giving back to the people the responsibility for those things they can do for themselves. The result will be a reinvigoration of deliberative politics at the state and local level that will draw the citizens back into the rough-and-tumble fray of political participation and the actual conduct of their affairs.

Such a notion of federalism is not an outdated relic of a distant past; the states still contribute to the vitality of American republicanism in ways no other arrangement could. In looking back at the main points of the Antifederalists' argument in behalf of small republics—to bolster the voluntary attachment of the people to the polity, to generate genuine responsibility of the government to the governed, and to nurture the moral development of the citizenry—we still find evidence to support their theoretical claims.

Certainly the states and communities afford the greatest opportunities to participate in government. From the lowest elective offices to the highest, from the various civic, charitable, and political associations that thrive at the state and local levels, there are places and opportunities for the ordinary citizen to engage in public affairs. By being less remote, states and communities are more accessible. It is far easier, for instance, to petition the local school board for a redress of grievances than it is to seek relief from Congress: the smaller the jurisdiction, the greater the clout of the individual.

It is at this level of community involvement, of political participation writ small, that the human being can truly feel himself to be a citizen. Because of this more intimate connection between the individual and the government, there tends to be a greater responsiveness and accountability of the governors to the governed. The louder the public voice, the more forceful the sentiment on the actions of those chosen to hold political power. Even the most casual glance at a campaign, for example, for a county commission reveals this to be true. Compared with the great national issues of presidential politics, such local battles may not be of much interest—at least to those outside the particular community. To those within the particular community, however, the issues of such elections are often far more pressing and interesting than any others. For these will tend to be the issues that touch the residents' lives most directly. The importance lies in the far more immediate consequences that will flow from the sorts of political choices involved. Such local political controversies are what knit a community together; public debate is the way public values are expressed; and public values are what make a collection of individuals into a community.

By attracting public attention and forcing people to take sides, public debate becomes an outlet for the moral sensibilities of the citizens, thus encouraging their moral development. For the most part local political battles are waged over what the community thinks it ought to be, rather than as mere exercises in shrewd politicking of the lowest sort. In a sense every public debate—from the fluoridation of the water supply to abortion and school prayer—touches basic moral questions about which citizens typically hold rather strong opinions. In being forced to address such questions as matters of public policy, people become practiced in thinking through tough moral choices. How much, for example, should a community spend on emergency life-saving equipment: how much is it worth to save a life? Is abortion an absolute wrong that should be prohibited across the board: should a twelve-year-old rape victim be forced to bear a child? Is pornography detrimental to the moral climate of the community: should publications such as *Playboy* and *Hustler* be banned? Are books—great literature—that use the language of racism a threat to civil liberties: should *Huckleberry Finn* be taken from the shelves of public libraries? Whatever one's views on such questions, public debate forces a person to hone his arguments and bring his deeply held

141

convictions into contact with others with similarly deeply held convictions on the other side.

Such debate becomes a kind of public education. All sides are aired; some opinions are confirmed, and others changed. And in the process the individual is enhanced for having had the obligation and the opportunity to puzzle through some of the most vexing issues of political life. This is precisely the sort of moral development and civic virtue the Antifederalists argued would result from a structure of government wherein the citizens felt themselves a part of the polity, where they believed the government was truly responsive and accountable to them.

This is the deepest understanding of those who still argue in behalf of federalism. The appeal is to that part of the American political tradition that began with the Antifederalists and the dedication to self-government. Thus the Antifederal tradition must be understood if we are to understand ourselves. For if the "foundation of the American polity was laid by the Federalists, the Antifederalist reservations echo through American history; and it is in the dialogue, not merely in the Federalist victory, that the country's principles are to be discovered."[60] As *A Federal Republican*, a spirited Antifederalist whose name has been lost in the mists of time, put it so long ago: "Whatever the refinements of modern politics may inculcate, it is still certain that some degree of virtue must exist, or freedom cannot live."[61]

Notes

1. Martin Diamond, *"The Federalist's* View of Federalism," in George C.S. Benson, ed., *Essays on Federalism* (Claremont, Calif.: 1961), p. 40.

2. Jacob E. Cooke, ed., *The Federalist* 51 (Middletown, Conn.: Wesleyan University Press, 1961), p. 353. All references are to this edition, hereafter cited as *The Federalist*.

3. James Curtis Ballagh, ed., *The Letters of Richard Henry Lee*, 2 vols. (New York: Macmillan, 1911), vol. 2, pp. 500 and 465. Hereafter cited as Ballagh.

4. *The Federalist* 1, p. 4.

5. Herbert J. Storing, ed., *The Complete Anti-Federalist*, 7 vols., (Chicago: University of Chicago Press, 1982), vol. 1, *What the Anti-Federalists Were For*, p. 10. All references to the various Antifederalist writers, unless otherwise noted, are to these volumes. References to the introduction, *What the Anti-Federalists Were For*, hereafter will be indicated by Storing; references to the various Antifederalists will be indicated by the author's name and the place in the volumes where the article appears, using Storing's method of annotation. For example, an article by the *Federal Farmer* would be indicated by 2.8.97, noting that the reference in question appears in the second volume of the collection, the eighth item in volume two, and the ninety-seventh paragraph of that essay.

I have drawn heavily from Storing's work on the Antifederalists and the "other" Federalists in constructing this essay. I have also, in certain areas, drawn liberally from my review of Storing's collection, "The Losers' Legacy," *The Virginia Quarterly Review* (Summer 1984), pp. 550–61.

6. See James Madison to George Washington, April 16, 1787: "Conceiving that an individual independence of the States is utterly irreconcileable with their aggregate sovereignty; and that *a consolidation of the whole into one simple republic would be as inexpedient as it is unattainable*, I have sought for some middle ground, which may at once support a due supremacy of the national authority, and not exclude the local authorities wherever they can be sub-ordinately useful" [emphasis supplied]. Robert A. Rutland et al., eds., *The Papers of James Madison* (Chicago: University of Chicago Press, 1975), vol. 9, p. 383.

7. Storing, p. 11. See also *The Federalist* 14.

8. See Herbert J. Storing, "The 'Other' Federalist Papers," *The Political Science Reviewer: 1976.*

9. *The Federalist* 6, p. 35.

10. Storing, p. 6

11. Ibid., p. 76. See William A. Schambra, "The Roots of the American Public Philosophy," *The Public Interest* (Spring 1982), pp. 36–48; and James Q. Wilson, *Thinking About Crime*, rev. ed. (New York: Basic Books, 1983), pp. 223–49.

12. Ibid., pp. 15–23.

13. *The Federal Farmer*, 2.8.24.

14. Ibid., 2.8.93.

15. Richard Henry Lee to _____, April 28, 1788, Ballagh, 2:464.

16. Storing, p. 42; and *The Federalist* 14 and 15.

17. See *The Federal Farmer*, 2.8.97.

18. Ibid., 2.8.101.

19. "The Address and Reasons of the Dissent of the Minority of the Con-vention of Pennsylvania to Their Constituents," 3.11.50; and *The Federalist* 15 and 17.

20. *Agrippa*, 4.6.48.

21. Richard Henry Lee, Ballagh, 2:464.

22. *The Impartial Examiner*, 5.14.8.

23. *The Federalist* 10, p.62.

24. Richard Henry Lee to Governor Edmund Randolph, October 16, 1787, 5.6.2

25. Melancton Smith, 6.12.7; Abraham Lincoln, "Address before the Young Men's Lyceum," Springfield, Illinois, January 27, 1838, in Gary L. McDowell, ed., *Taking the Constitution Seriously* (Dubuque: Kendall-Hunt, 1981), p.469.

26. *The Federalist* 10, pp. 57 and 65; and *The Federal Farmer*, 2.8.6.

27. Richard Henry Lee, 5.6.1.

28. Melancton Smith, 6.12.15.

29. *The Federal Farmer*, 2.8.15.

30. Ibid., 2.8.158.

31. Melancton Smith, 6.12.18.

32. Storing, p. 18.
33. *The Federal Farmer*, 2.8.158.
34. Ibid., 2.8.163.
35. Melancton Smith, 6.12.20.
36. *Brutus*, 2.9.16.
37. *Cato*, 2.6.34; Storing, p. 20.
38. *A [Maryland] Farmer*, 5.1.82; *The Impartial Examiner*, 5.14.6.
39. Charles Turner, 4.18.1
40. *Cato*, 2.6.34.
41. *Alfred*, 3.10.5.
42. See Storing, p. 39; Caroline Robbins, *The Eighteenth Century Common-wealthman* (Cambridge: Harvard University Press, 1959).
43. John Clive and Bernard Bailyn, "England's Cultural Provinces: Scotland and America," *The William and Mary Quarterly* 11 (1954), pp. 200–43.
44. See Istvan Hont and Michael Ignatieff, eds., *Wealth & Virtue: The Shaping of Political Economy in the Scottish Enlightenment* (Cambridge: Cambridge University Press, 1984).
45. Duncan Forbes, introduction to Adam Ferguson, *An Essay on the History of Civil Society* (Edinburgh: Edinburgh University Press, 1966), p. xiii. All references to Ferguson are to this edition, herefter cited as *Essay*.
46. Douglass Adair, " 'That Politics May Be Reduced to A Science': David Hume, James Madison, and the Tenth Federalist," *Huntington Library Quarterly*, vol. 20 (1957), pp. 343–60.
47. Ferguson, *Essay*, p. 225. For a more detailed discussion of Ferguson's constitutionalism, see Gary L. McDowell, "Commerce, Virtue, and Politics: Adam Ferguson's Constitutionalism," *The Review of Politics*, vol. 45 (1983), pp. 536–52.
48. Ferguson, *Essay*, p. 237.
49. Ibid., pp. 143; 236–43.
50. Ibid., p. 254.
51. Ibid., p. 165.
52. Ibid., pp. 271–72.
53. See James Madison's list of books for use by Congress, William T. Hutchinson, et al., eds., *The Papers of James Madison* (Chicago: University of Chicago Press, 1969), vol. 6, pp. 66 and 86.
54. "The Fallacies of the Freeman Detected by *A Farmer*," 3.14.7.
55. Richard Henry Lee to George Mason, May 15, 1787, Ballagh, 2:419.
56. Storing, p. 16.
57. It has been argued that the "happy relation of States to Nation [constitutes] our central political problem." Felix Frankfurter and James Landis, *The Business of the Supreme Court* (New York: Macmillan, 1929), p. 2.
58. Alexis de Tocqueville, *Democracy in America*, ed. J.P. Mayer (New York: Harper & Row, 1969), p. 44.
59. *Ibid.*, p. 95.
60. Storing, p. 3.
61. *A Federal Republican*, 3.6.21.